TASTE AND SEE

Also by Margaret Silf

LANDMARKS: AN IGNATIAN JOURNEY

THE MILLER'S TALE
(published by Avon Books)

TASTE AND SEE

ADVENTURING INTO PRAYER

MARGARET SILF

with illustrations by **ROY LOVATT**

DARTON · LONGMAN + TODD

First published in 1999 by
Darton, Longman and Todd Ltd
1 Spencer Court
140–142 Wandsworth High Street
London SW18 4JJ

ISBN 0–232–52318–5

A catalogue record for this book is available from the British Library.

Scripture quotations are taken from the Jerusalem Bible, published and copyright 1966,
1967 and 1968 by Darton, Longman and Todd Ltd and Doubleday & Co. Inc.

Designed and produced by Sandie Boccacci
using QuarkXPress on an Apple PowerMac 7500
Set in 11/14pt Bembo
Printed and bound in Great Britain by
Page Bros, Norwich, Norfolk

"How good Yahweh is —
only taste and see!"

(Psalm 34:8)

CONTENTS

PREFACE: A hole in the wall

For most of my life, I see now with hindsight, there was a large and solid wall, firmly dividing my experience of God from my experience of every-day living. God, as far as he figured at all in my scheme of things, was 'Sunday business' and the business of Monday to Saturday had a consider-ably bigger share of my attention. Even when I started to grow more aware of spiritual things and take God more seriously, all that happened was that this inner wall shifted a bit, and the God-side of it expanded while the 'world' side shrank in significance.

How wrong can you be? I began to find out how wrong I was being when someone did a very simple thing: He (very gently) removed a brick from my 'wall'. I hardly noticed the operation at the time, but I noticed its effects! All at once I could see the other side. Whichever side I happened to be standing on at any given time, it was always possible to see through this wondrous hole in the wall. And it was impossible to keep Sunday away from weekdays any more. From then on I couldn't keep God out of my world, my everyday, my business. Nor could I keep my everyday out of God's way. The defences were breached, and the wall that had seemed so solid and fixed turned out to be just a flimsy divider that had its foundations in my own mind.

My search for God, from then on, could not be separated from my everyday living. I realised increasingly that God's search for me, and for all of us, was taking place in every aspect of lived experience. Not a single choice or action or relationship could be made or lived out outside of the light of God that was streaming through the hole my friend had made. And all he did to make the hole was to point out the genuine connection between very specific things that were happening in my life, and some of the strands of my longing and searching for meaning, for truth and for God. He placed these two threads in my hand, side by side, the thread of faith and the thread of life, and together we let God begin his weaving.

My hope and prayer is that the reflections shared in this book will help to remove a few bricks from that flimsy, but so unyielding wall that separates our journeys in faith from our journeys through daily life. This is an adventure into prayer which will call us to pass freely and frequently backwards and forwards across the boundaries of 'prayer' and 'life' until we find that there never was a boundary, except in our own perceptions.

I recently heard it said that 'we inherit far more than we ever create'. The legacy that I have inherited is huge and can never be adequately acknowledged. I would, however, like to express my deepest gratitude to: Brian McClorry, for removing that first crucial brick, for encouraging me to explore both sides of the 'wall', and for supporting my often wayward wanderings with patience and unfailing encouragement; to Gerry Hughes for the precious gift of his personal companionship on my journey and for the deep well of his wisdom and experience from which he allows me to draw so freely; to Teresa Foster who walks so many gritty paths with me and never fails to direct my gaze to the diamonds among the stones.

My warmest thanks go also to my husband Klaus and daughter Kirstin who are so often the first revealers of God's action in our everyday living, and give me so much support and encouragement in so many ways – and to those cherished friends, who know who they are, who have been my soul-companions through the years, especially my friends from the Christian communities at Keele University and in the neighbourhood of Stoke-on-Trent. My gratitude goes very specially to those who have allowed me to share something of their stories in these pages.

I first began to write the material in this book in response to requests from groups of Christians seeking to deepen their life of prayer, and so I would like to thank those groups particularly for their welcoming openness, their infectious enthusiasm and their ongoing friendship. I thank especially the people of St Michael's, St Margaret's, St Andrew's and St Barnabus' in Stoke-on-Trent, and the people of St John the Baptist in Tamworth.

Thus the friends of our living become the friends in our believing, and the wall that divides us from God and from each other gradually crumbles. I thank all who have shared with me their journeys of faith-in-life and life-in-faith. They have allowed me to walk with them upon their personal holy ground, and there is no greater gift that we can give each other than that. And I thank all who have inspired in me the trust to share my own journeying with *them*. Stories and resonances from many of these journeys pervade the pages of this book. They stream through the holes in our walls and dissolve our demarcations. Perhaps the cover illustration shows something of this process in action: a heart opening to God and also open to all the colours of the world. This is the dynamic of prayer that this book explores.

But there is a long road stretching between the thoughts and feelings of prayer, and the pages of a book. I would like to thank those who have built this road: Morag Reeve, Helen Porter and Allison Ward, and all friends and colleagues at Darton, Longman and Todd for their hard work and unfailing encouragement, Roy Lovatt for the skill and vision embodied in his illustrations, Peter McClure for his skilful lettering, and Sarah John for the beautiful cover design.

Walls for breaking through, and roads for re-connecting – my thanks go to everyone, in time or eternity, who has removed barriers, opened gateways and travelled roads with me.

A FEAST OF RAINBOWS

A friend once took me by surprise when he invited me to look at a special gift he had received. I followed him into his room, and over to the window. There he showed me a small crystal pendant suspended from the ceiling. It could easily have been overlooked. I would certainly never have noticed it had he not pointed it out to me and told me about the friend who had sent it to him.

At first I really didn't know what to say or how to react. The pendant just hung there, lifelessly, and I wasn't sure that I could see what he saw in it. Then, ever so gently, he touched it slightly with the tip of his finger, and it began to swing. *Then* I saw the point! Suddenly the whole room was alive with dancing light – a feast of rainbows circling through the darkest corners of the room and spreading out to fill the ceiling with light and colour.

He was a man of mature years and acknowledged wisdom, not a person to be lightly carried away on a whim, but I saw his eyes light up in delight as he touched the crystal into life. I saw the joy of a child seeing the world for the very first time – or the joy of a creator who has found a means of vibrant self-expression. And the joy was infectious. I felt as though I had been present to a miracle.

A miracle ... and also a sacrament of prayer? A heart that is focused on God is like that crystal hanging silently from the ceiling. It does nothing in itself, except to be what it is. But it is open to the full radiance of the morning light, such as streamed in through my friend's window. It is open and receptive to an invisible light. And when it is touched into motion, it breaks down this invisible light into all the colours of the world. The 'light inaccessible, hid from our eyes' of which the hymn speaks, becomes accessible and visible. It reveals itself in every colour and shade of our lived experience, and in the infinite variations of our everyday. It calls us, personally, to be in touch with the heart of the creator, and to let his light be expressed in the colours of our lives. It calls us into Life.

A lovely thought, but does it really *mean* anything in our all too tedious struggles with prayer? Only this, perhaps: the pendant didn't have to do anything except be focused towards the light and permit the touch that nudged it into life. Maybe that gives us a clue about our own attempts to pray?

The material in this book was originally written for various groups of people who said they were looking for ways of being in a more personal relationship with God through prayer. This desire, in itself, was enough to focus their hearts towards the light they were seeking. When you picked up this book and began to read it, you were expressing the same kind of desire. Such desire is all God needs to start revealing his infinite variety in our lives and in our world.

Once this initial desire had brought them together to share their journeying and their searching, all they needed to do was to be themselves, receptive to the nudging of God in their hearts. No more is asked of you. Simply be open to the possibilities of the feast. All you need, to gain admission, is a sense of wonder, and the kind of trust that takes the presence of God seriously in every choice you make and in every event that presents itself in your life.

To take God seriously is, sooner or later, going to call us to trust his guidance in making the many choices – some of them life-changing – that arise in our daily lives. If God is asking us to direct our lives, minute by minute, in the light of his guidance, how can we be *sure* of that guidance? For most, such certainty is not part of our mental and emotional experience. We tend to look with scepticism upon those who claim to have divine revelations. We regard such people as either spiritual giants, or fools.

This book isn't for either spiritual giants or for fools. (Except that, if we are honest, most of us have moments when our hearts soar to the mountain tops and make us feel that we alone among humankind have glimpsed the meaning of the universe, and most of us feel a little bit foolish afterwards!) Prayer, surely, is not a haven of certainty, but a way of being in uncertainty. So this book is for those who know that they don't know, but have enough trust in their hearts to take the first steps of prayer and see where it leads them. I am taking these steps, these first steps, myself, and I expect still to be taking first steps on the day I die. I invite you to discover your own steps and let God build up your confidence, gradually and steadily, that this, truly, is a path that can be trusted.

If this book isn't for spiritual giants, just as certainly it isn't for 'religious' people either. If prayer is meaningful at all, it is meaningful for everyone. I remember an evening of faith-sharing I was once involved with. The participants came from various parts of Liverpool. They worked in shops, factories, schools and homes, or, in several cases, they had no jobs at all. They were all trying to let prayer become a reality in their lives.

One evening, when they had been reflecting, during the week, on Jesus' description of himself as 'the true vine', they were sharing their feelings. One lady, who worked twelve hours a day, six days a week in a back-street greengrocer's shop, admitted shyly that she simply had found no time at all for quiet 'prayer'. Even her brief lunch breaks were always in the presence of her colleagues. Contemplation, in any accepted sense, was clearly an impossibility in the reality of her daily life. Her short and busy evenings were organised around the needs of her young family. Where was prayer supposed to fit in?

For ten minutes or so I listened to the story of her day and her week, and I heard the unspoken sadness and frustration that prayer seemed to her to be out of reach. Then she hesitated for a moment. Her eyes began to shine a little. And, a little sheepishly perhaps, she told me about her meeting with the grapes. She described the grapes lying in the crate on a shelf in the shop, and hanging from hooks on the wall.

'Suddenly,' she said, 'I remembered Jesus' words. I kept looking at the grapes. They were so inviting, so juicy and so *different*. No two grapes were quite the same size or shape, texture or colour. And I thought – we are like that. Each of us a different grape on God's vine, each with our own special flavour.'

She went on to tell me how, once the thought had occurred to her, she went through the week with frequent glances at the grapes to relive the moment when she had first noticed God in them. That moment of insight was prayer – God's greeting to her in the greengrocer's shop. And her continued returning to the graced moment was prayer too – her response to God's greeting. And so, as she came to recognise, and to trust, God was becoming ever more vividly present to her daily work and her frustration began to change into gladness and expectancy.

Another friend, who had decided one year to set Advent aside as a time for deeper personal prayer, found that her small daughter had other ideas. The child wanted, so very much, to have a 'Big Ears' to go with her 'Noddy'. This was her sole wish for Christmas, but her mother trawled through the toyshops in vain, and in the end decided that she would have to knit a Big Ears herself for her little daughter.

And so the precious prayer time became more and more curtailed as Christmas approached and the Big Ears project took over. She barely knew where to start, but she gathered all kinds of scraps of wool from around the house and from friends and relatives, and then she used her imagination, hoping that the resulting toy would meet with her daughter's approval on Christmas morning. Prayer too became a daily search for meaning in an overloaded schedule in the service of her family, and the hope that God would accept the results.

When the big day came she knew that her efforts had been fruitful. Her daughter showed Big Ears to everyone she met, with the proud and joyful introduction: 'This is Big Ears and my mummy knitted him herself!' The toy meant so much more to her than any machine-made equivalent that the shops might have stocked.

'Mum' told me this story, full of regret for the 'prayer' she had failed to make during Advent. But what I heard wasn't her regret, but God's delight over all she had discovered of him, of love and of life during these weeks of preparation for another Child. She had gathered the scraps of her experience into her living prayer during that time, just as surely as she had gathered the scraps of wool for Big Ears, and there was no doubt in my mind that God was sharing the story with the angels and saints, with the proud words: 'This is prayer, and she knitted it herself!' Surely he rejoiced more over that home-made Advent prayer than over the formal retreat that she never made!

There is more prayer in the scrap-yards of our hearts than we imagine. If we look for signs in the heavens, we may easily overlook God's footprints in the High Street. The true vine is on the greengrocer's shelf. The pearl of great price lies hidden in the cracks of the paving stones we walk. And the salt of the earth is what we sprinkle on our own potatoes.

The purpose of this book is to explore some ways of becoming more aware of 'God's footprints in the High Street.' It is an invitation to the 'feast of rainbows' that swings into motion when God touches your heart with the desire for prayer. An invitation to the feast spread out for you in your own heart, where God himself invites you to 'taste and see' for yourself some of the very many ways that you may find helpful in coming closer to him in your personal prayer.

The book is divided into four sections.

'*Approaches*' looks at some guiding principles for the journey of personal prayer: the discovery of God's life-generating presence within our own hearts and lived experience; the call to stillness; the positive power of our own desires, and the art of living reflectively, so that what is discovered in the stillness of heart that we call prayer can become effective in the reality of everyday life.

'*Focusing the telescope*' does a little 'nudging', to bring your pendant-heart into motion in particular, and specific ways. These are some ways of engaging in personal prayer that you may find helpful. Try them, and see whether they bring any new light into your lived experience.

'*The Word made prayer*' explores ways of praying with Scripture – ways in which God's Word itself can be the 'nudge' that draws you into prayer.

'*Stumbling blocks and stepping stones*' offers a few thoughts on overcoming some of the difficulties and making use of some opportunities in the journey into prayer, and of letting prayer become a way of life.

Each of these sections comprises several short chapters, each exploring one way of approaching personal prayer. Each chapter is also accompanied by suggestions for exercises in 'taking it further', and by an illustration which may help to lead you into your own meditation along the ways suggested in the chapter.

Some of these ways of prayer may be appealing to you; others less so. I suggest that you begin by reflecting on the foundations suggested in Part 1. Then explore for yourself the various possibilities set out in the remainder of the book. Take and use anything you find helpful, and leave the rest aside. And bear in mind that there is an infinite number of ways of praying. No one way is ever 'the right way' or 'the only way'. What is right for you is what draws you closer to God and to your truest self, at this particular time and place of your journey. The approaches suggested here are merely the ones I myself have found helpful so far in my own journey. I make no apology for the many omissions, because I can only share what I have experienced myself.

Above all, these 'recipes for prayer' have one thing in common: they all make use of ingredients that you will find readily to hand in the life you are living day by day. All you need to try them for yourself is an attentive awareness of your day-by-day experience, together with a real desire to seek God in that experience. The results will give you bread for your journey: bread to nourish your continual growth towards God who is at the heart of all you are, and, perhaps, bread to share with others.

God feeds us continually from the feast of himself that is evident everywhere around us, if we journey with open eyes. He invites us to taste and see how good he is, and what a joy prayer can be, and then to reflect that joy around the place in which we live, as the dancing pendant filled the room with light and life and colour.

PART ONE
APPROACHES

Prayer invites us into the possibility of a living interaction between the transcendent God who will remain always beyond all we can think or imagine, and the immanent God who abides deep within our own hearts.

How can we open ourselves up to this possibility? How might we approach this call, this desire in our own hearts and in God's, for a personal relationship with the one who is closer to us than we are to ourselves, and whose dream of us is coming to birth in all the days of our lives?

This section suggests some ways of entering upon a journey of prayer.

1. The broad bean and the blotting paper
Discovering the God inside

2. Tuning in to God
Prayer as listening

3. Sinking into silence
Ways towards inner stillness

4. Reflecting, connecting
The bridge between prayer and daily life

5. What are you looking for?
Focusing on what we really desire

1. THE BROAD BEAN AND THE BLOTTING PAPER

Discovering the God inside

I remember the day, many moons ago, when I was introduced to the secret of life . . . .

It was all so simple, and the simplicity of it comes back to me today as a model worth following as we begin this journey of exploration together.

It began with an instruction to bring a jam-jar and a piece of blotting paper from home to our next science lesson in primary school. In those days jam-jars weren't thrown into the bottle bank, but were washed and stored in the cellar, and re-cycled in the kitchen every strawberry season. And blotting paper was a household necessity in the days of pen and ink. So it wasn't much to ask, and most children could easily comply with the request.

Once our rows of jam-jars were assembled in the classroom, the miracle could begin. We were told to soak our sheets of blotting paper with tap water and place them as a lining round the inside of our jam-jars. We were still at the age of wonder, and no-one had spoiled the story for us by telling us the plot in advance. The science teacher came round and gave each of us a broad bean, which was clearly going to play some key role in the unfolding drama. We were then invited to place our beans carefully between the wet blotting paper and the inside surface of our jam-jar.

And that, really, was the end of all demands upon us. The little trinity of offerings was prepared – the jar, the wet blotting paper and the broad bean – and the rest was out of our hands . . . .

What happened next was nothing, really. All the teacher did was to line up our jam-jars along the window-sill, strategically positioned above the central heating radiators, and in the full light of the morning sun. And then we left the experiment to get on with itself.

Everyone knows the rest of the story. A week later, when we re-visited our jam-jars, of course each bean had sprouted. Perhaps there is never

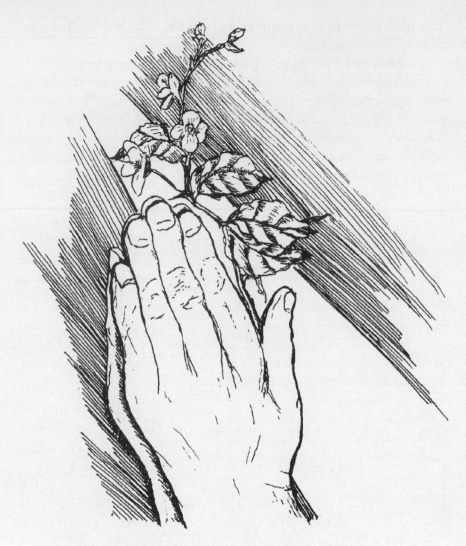

We bring ourselves and
our experience
  into the light of prayer,
and let the Lifemaker
  do the rest.

again quite the thrill of that experiment, when we first observe the beginnings of new life with our own eyes, and in our own jam-jars.

The more I think about it, the more it reminds me of prayer . . . .

If we are willing to think small, it isn't too hard to see our day-by-day lived experience as a piece of blotting paper, soaking up impressions, reactions, events, demands, responses. And the blotting paper of our lived experience sits (comfortably or otherwise) within our world, the jam-jar.

Then comes the bean – the seed of our own uniqueness that will grow into our personal individual being, and which is the dream God dreams of us when his love spills over into creation. Our Godseed. Dry and dormant, maybe for many a long year, but one day the moment comes – the 'kairos moment', God's perfect timing, when our lived experience, soaked through with the living water of the Holy Spirit, starts to sprout, and begins its amazing growth into 'Who-I-Am'.

And all we have done is to bring our threefold offering to the place of miracle (which is wherever we happen to find ourselves). We bring our Godseed, our lived experience and our world, and let the Lifemaker do the rest.

Yet we can *help* the process, both in ourselves, and in others. Just as the primary school teacher lined up our bean-jars along the window-sill above the radiators, where they would enjoy both warmth and light, so we can bring our raw ingredients to the place of warmth and light.

When it comes to kindling the desire for prayer, and encouraging its growth, warmth means an accepting, encouraging and safe space. We give warmth when we 'befriend' the desires of our heart, accepting them just as they are, and letting them come to consciousness, welcoming ourselves without judgement or denial or reproach. And we give warmth when we walk alongside others, listening with love and awe as they reveal *their* heart's deepest desires and inner movements, trusting that we will understand, accept and affirm. Heart speaks to heart only where there is such warmth.

And light? Well if there is any light to be shed it is not our own. We are like the planets, generating no light of our own, yet able, and called, to *reflect* the light of our creator. This reflected light is also needed if the broad bean is to come to life. Some of this light comes to us through the prayer-wisdom and practice of the centuries, that has illumined so many pilgrim paths before our own. We can never teach ourselves, or others, to pray, because prayer is gift, but we *can* receive the light passed on to us from those who have made the journey of prayer ahead of us, and we, in our turn, can pass on something of that light to those who follow after. And we can pass it on in the language and the images of our own times and of our own generation's experience of the world.

The light, whether it comes directly from God to the praying heart, or whether it is reflected light shared by fellow pilgrims, reaches our Godseed through the glass of the jam-jar. It travels to our hearts through the reality of the created world. The Godseed sprouts and grows right there in the blotting paper of our own lived experience, where it has its roots. The various approaches to prayer that we will be exploring together are firmly grounded in these two places: in our *world* and in our *lived experience*. And they are brought to life by the gifts of warmth and light: gifts that we receive from God, but that we also give to each other, and to ourselves.

Given these conditions, we, like those seven-year-olds all those years ago, will find ourselves once more on the threshold of the secret of life. But this time the life that we will see sprouting is the eternal life that God is calling into fullness in our hearts. Prayer, rooted firmly in *where-we-are*, yet striving for *where-we-long-to-be*, is the expression of that heart-call – God's call to us, and our response.

And it is so very *simple*. We can see the miracle with our own eyes. We can watch it happening in our own jam-jars. And once we have seen its beginnings in the depths of our own hearts, and started to notice its effects in the way we live and relate to each other, we will know that we have touched into the secret of Life.

The purpose of this book is to offer a little warmth and a little light. The jam-jar is all around us, in the created world in which we live, and the political world in which we operate, with all its glory and its shame. You yourself will need to bring along the blotting paper of your daily lived experience, soaked as it already is, with the living water of God's Spirit that has been springing within you since your life began. And your Godseed, of course – the broad bean that is uniquely and irreplaceably *you*, among all the other 57 times 57 varieties – the Godseed which is already sprouting and striving for all that it is becoming, in God.

Equipped with these raw materials, we might explore together some ways of adventuring into personal prayer, enjoying the warmth of good companionship as we journey, and letting a little light shine in still undiscovered places.

TAKING IT FURTHER ...

I once heard it said that 'truth is delivered to us daily, fresh-baked in the ovens of our own experience'. Just reflect quietly on the picture that these words evoke for you. Try making friends with your 'oven' – the everyday experience that can sometimes feel like a prison or a hamster's wheel, and sometimes like a roller coaster ride. Reflect on the possibility that the walls that seem to enclose you, the heat and frenzy that seem to stifle you, and the delays and frustrations that seem to hold you back, may be the very means of baking the bread of your truth in the oven of your experience.

Just let yourself be still for five or ten minutes, alone if possible, in a place where you feel comfortable. Relax, and simply *enjoy* this time of being *you*, free for a while of the many demands on you by other people or circumstances to fit into *their* plans and structures. Let yourself be like the broad bean, whose only purpose is to grow into what it really is, to sprout, and to discover its own unique fruitfulness.

When you reflect on this innermost kernel of yourself, that contains your unique, eternal blueprint in itself, can you recognise what, or who is providing, or has ever provided warmth and light to bring your real you to life and growth? Perhaps you recall particular times and places that have made you feel especially alive, or particular people who may (perhaps quite unconsciously) have spoken a word, or sparked an idea or response in you which now, with hindsight, you can see was life-giving, or even life-changing.

Let your memories float free. Enjoy them. Draw, once more, on the energy that they have released in you. Pack them in your inner 'rucksack', as food for the journey that we are about to begin.

2. TUNING IN TO GOD

Prayer as listening

Receiving or transmitting?

On my way to work I pass the radio telescope at Jodrell Bank. Every time I pass, it seems to be in a different position – sometimes flat, with its huge dish raised to the skies like a soup bowl, sometimes almost upright, as if searching out some stray star that is just about to slip beyond the horizon. Sometimes I see it actually moving, and its huge bulk creaks heavily up or down, left or right. It all looks very laboured.

Whenever I pass Jodrell Bank, it reminds me of prayer. Prayer can be pretty heavy-going too. At least, it often seems like that, especially if we go at it in the ways that we have so often, traditionally, been taught as children. Do you remember those last five minutes at infant school, before the going-home bell rang? The 'hands together, eyes closed' time, while you screwed up your face and tried to squint through your eyelids to see what everyone else was doing, while the class chanted something that went vaguely over your head without making much impression on your heart?

Depending on your Christian tradition, you may also have learned that, to be effective, prayer must be painful. Stiff limbs and aching knees were part of the package, and the rest was often a test of memory. And perhaps the worst of all was the awful sense of guilt that overcame you when you forgot, or wilfully omitted, your prayers, or found, at the end of a time of prayer, that you had been away with the fairies and couldn't even rightly remember what you had said.

But perhaps, in all of this, I am in danger of projecting my own short-comings onto you. Maybe your early experience of prayer was entirely satisfactory – a child who learns to pray in a parent's embrace, for example, has a head start when it comes to relating to a loving God. But however you learned to pray, you will have your own reasons for picking up this book and looking, perhaps, for fresh ways and a new vision, in your personal journey with God.

Whatever those reasons are, I would just like to begin by inviting you

Listening, receiving, coming to rest in the direction of God.

back to Jodrell Bank, because I think that it can show us a way to pray. A radio telescope reminds me of the huge, complicated efforts we make to 'catch the signals of the stars'. But it also shows me a profound truth. It reminds me that all we can really do, to 'receive' God, is to direct our hearts towards him, and trust him to do the rest. It spells out for me a few simple ground rules:

- That prayer is *God's initiative*, not our achievement.
- That prayer is about *listening*, more than about talking.
- That prayer is about *receiving*, more than about asking for.
- That prayer is about *coming to rest in the direction of God*.

The radio telescope can do nothing more than direct itself towards the source of the signal. It can't force the signal to happen. All its efforts are directed towards receiving the signal and interpreting it in ways that mean something for life on earth. And prayer too is like that. We can open ourselves up to it, and remain alert to it. We can receive it, and reflect on what it means for our daily living. We can act on it, and let it inform our choices and decisions. But we cannot force it, because prayer is *God's gift*, and, however carefully we prepare for it, it will always take us by surprise, which, after all, is what real gifts are supposed to do!

And how might we set about opening ourselves up to 'receive' God in this sort of way? I would suggest that we do this in exactly the same way as we would open our hearts to a dear friend who had something to share with us. We *listen*. And we ask for the grace to listen with our full attention, and with the trust and expectation that we would have in a conversation with our friend . . . . And to listen like this requires a degree of stillness and silence that doesn't always come naturally in our world of feverish and anxious activity and 'busy-ness'.

Ten feet down

A friend once told me an interesting fact that if you can imagine yourself in a stormy sea, and then imagine yourself ten feet below the trough of the highest wave, the water would be perfectly calm. The picture appealed to me, and helps me to come to prayer.

Like most people, I live most of my life on the 'surface' of myself. My conscious journey through a typical day is mainly occupied with the 'waves'. Sometimes they are manageable. Sometimes they reach storm force and at the end of the day I feel exhausted and fraught. Yet this stillness, if my friend is right, lies just 'ten feet down'. That doesn't seem like an impossible depth to reach. Might it not be a way of reaching the stillness of heart in which prayer can happen?

Through the ages, men and women have always sought this close communion with God, that we call prayer, and almost all traditions of faith and spiritual searching have realised that prayer depends on stillness. The purpose of stilling ourselves is to bring us down to the deeper currents of our hearts, where we can begin to notice what we are really feeling, what is moving us at a deeper level of our being, and where these feelings and movements have their roots. And it is precisely in those deep currents that God is speaking to our hearts, revealing our innermost desires and fears to us, inviting us to reach out towards the deepest desire of our hearts and to surrender our fears and hurts to his healing . . . .

. . . Surrender! A challenging word, and an act of faith in itself. Because when we still ourselves and sink 'ten feet down', we are acknowledging that we are not our own managers, and that our surface thoughts and pre-occupations, and even our images of God and notions of 'how prayer ought to be', can be obstacles to our meeting with God in the deepest reaches of ourselves. Prayer is an act of surrender. It asks us to let go of our own agenda, and listen to God. It involves risk.

When we surrender, we take a risk. We make ourselves open to God's suggestions. We do so in an act of faith, trusting that he will pour himself into our stillness, and fill us with his Spirit. When this happens, we can no more predict the consequences, than the astronomer can specify in advance what the skies will reveal through the telescope, and what implications those revelations may have for life on earth. This is the cost, and the adventure, of the inner journey.

Tuning in

Once it is in the right position, the telescope becomes passive – simply waiting there, open and receptive. There is really only one active moment in this whole procedure – it needs to be *focused* on the place where the signal is expected to be found. This question of focusing lies, I believe, at the heart of prayer. When you are engaged in an intimate conversation with a friend, you will probably not be gazing out of the window, or concentrating on the state of your finger nails, or reading the newspaper. Much more probably you will be looking at your friend, and in eye-to-eye contact. And you won't even be aware that you are focusing so deeply on your friend, because your attention is no longer on *yourself*, and on how well you are doing in the interchange, but on your friend and what he or she is revealing to you.

And this is really quite a fundamental difference between the ways we have often learned to pray, and the kind of prayer that is truly directed towards God. Prayer that centres around 'my words', 'my petitions', 'what I want God to do for me', is all *me-centred*. Prayer that sinks into stillness and surrenders to God is *God-centred*. This book suggests some ways of coming to this deep stillness, and explores some ways of focusing our hearts on God. And we may discover that we are no longer 'saying our prayers', but, rather, *listening* to them.

As we sink into this focused stillness, the teeming questions that normally fill our minds are gradually relinquished as our own efforts lessen and our receptiveness sharpens. No longer: 'Where am I? What is happening to me? How must I do things?' But, simply:

'Be still, and know that I am God.'

TAKING IT FURTHER . . .

Finding a sacred space

At this early stage in our journey the most important thing is the discovery of our own inner stillness. This is the quiet place in our hearts where God can speak to us and where we can begin to listen and to hear.

Try remembering a place and a time where you have been deeply happy and contented and at peace. Let the scene come back to you. Remember where it was, what the weather was like, what season of the year. Were you alone, or with someone else? Feel the sun, or the rain again on your cheeks. Smell the scents of the place again. Hear its sounds. Go back there in your imagination, quite deliberately, and be quiet with your memories for a few minutes. In your own way, express your gratitude to God for this remembered experience. Invite him to come to you again in that memory, and to make that place a *sacred space* for you. A sacred space is quite simply a space where you can become more fully aware of God's presence with you.

These few minutes that you have spent with your memory *are* prayer. Be still, in the recognition that you have met God in your sacred space. Your 'inner telescope' has come to rest in a place where it feels focused on God. Perhaps you have come into this journey thinking 'I can't pray'. Now savour the joy of discovering that you *can* pray, and that it didn't hurt at all!

Now that you have discovered a 'sacred space' in your memory and in your heart, return to it as often as you feel drawn to do so. This could be in a quiet time of reflection, or it could be on the bus going to work, or in the queue at the supermarket checkout, or over the kitchen sink. Just go back to your 'space', but as you do so, ask God to meet you there. He is the One who first gave you the gift of the experience that you have remembered. Show him your joy in receiving it. Your own joy is only a fraction of *his* joy in receiving your response. If you doubt this, remember how you feel when you have given a child a Christmas gift and the child shows obvious happiness in the gift. Whose joy is greater – yours, the giver, or the child's?

If you practise this stilling exercise whenever you can, you will start to notice that, in all of the frenzy, there will be little pockets of calm. Your days will have been touched by prayer. Depending on your personal circumstances, you might like to find a corner of your home, or maybe another spot where you feel at ease and where you can be alone. If you can, make this little corner, physically, into a 'prayer space' – perhaps having a candle there, or a cross, or picture or some flowers and your Bible. This will become your focal point for setting aside a time of prayer in a special place.

But don't worry if this doesn't seem to be possible. Not all families offer individual family members the luxury of this kind of privacy! If this isn't for you, there are many other ways of marking a place in your life as 'prayer space'. Try putting some small reminder of your desire for God in the car, or on your desk at work, or in the kitchen with the detergents, or on the bathroom shelf. It doesn't have to be anything 'religious'. It may be much more powerful as a symbol if it is something that expresses your personal relationship with God.

As an example, my daughter gave me a little string hammock with a furry toy lying in it as a birthday present one year. I have it hanging on the window by my desk. Other people just see it as a toy, but for me it is a reminder that I am held in God's unfailing love, and when things get fraught, it reminds me that all I really need to do is to return to my awareness of that 'holding'. Little things like this are ways of returning to 'prayer' over and over again, right in the middle of life as we are actually living it.

Focusing the 'telescope'

This second exercise is intended to help you turn the 'dish' of your inner telescope towards God (and, therefore, away from yourself). This sounds so easy, but in practice, if you become aware of what is happening as you go through your daily life, you will realise that it is very difficult indeed to wrench the focus away from 'self', and towards the 'other', whether the 'other' is God or another human person.

It is hard, because it means coming face to face with the unpleasant fact that we all tend to relate to others in terms of how they are affecting us. Some people 'make us feel good', some disturb us, annoy us, antagonise us. Some seem well-meaning (but what are their motives?), others seem to want to undermine us. If we look at these sort of feelings towards others, we have to admit, in all honesty, that they are about 'how *I* feel'. They are not about how the other person feels.

The word 'empathy' is, I believe, about making that radical switch of focus from 'I' to the 'other'. If we can really feel as the other feels, if, as the Indians say, we can 'walk a mile in his moccasins', *then* we are *beginning* to learn to focus our hearts and to love with God's love. And empathy lies at the heart of all true listening. So the exercise is this:

Try noticing one or two of the conversations or encounters you have each day with another person. It doesn't matter whether they are friendly or not-so-friendly. Just become *aware* of them in a deliberate way. With practice you may be able to develop this awareness at the time of the conversation, but begin at least, by reflecting on one or two encounters each day before you go to sleep. Then ask yourself: 'Where was my focus, for the most part, during this conversation? On myself or on the other person?' But a word of warning – don't be discouraged if you find over and over again that the focus is mainly on yourself. That is how we human beings are, so, welcome to the human race! Almost no one practises real empathy in their dealings with others. But we can *learn* to do so, and our finest teacher is Jesus.

Try reflecting on one or two of these Gospel incidents, and let Jesus show you how *he* relates to others; notice especially where his *focus* is in these conversations:

- Matthew 14:22–33 (Jesus walks on the water: notice what happens to Peter's focus here.)
- Matthew 19:13–15 (Jesus with the little children. Where is Jesus' focus? Where is the focus of the disciples?)
- Luke 18:35–43 (Where is the blind man's focus? How does Jesus change

this? Reflect especially on the words 'What do you want me to do for you?')

Is there a relationship in your life where you feel there *is* true empathy (at least from time to time)? In the better moments of family life, a parent may, for example, notice that he or she is genuinely feeling the pain or the joy of a child, or of an elderly relative, and in doing so, is able to go beyond, or 'rise above' his or her own smaller interests. John the Baptist realises this need for complete 're-focusing', when he says (in John 3:30):

> *'He must grow greater,*
> *I must grow less'*

Find and treasure any moments of real empathy in your daily experience – your empathy with another, or another person's empathy with *you*, and *ask God to imprint on your heart how it feels when you are relating to another person in this way.* You may, for example, discover gifts in the day like the phone call from someone who really cares, to ask how you are, or that lurch of pain inside you when you hear a child being unjustly harangued by an overwrought parent. Such moments are pointers to empathy, to genuine 'holy listening'. They are pointers to the heart of God.

3. SINKING INTO SILENCE

Ways towards inner stillness

Ten feet down – that magic depth that my friend suggested to me as the place where the water is still – might as well be on another planet for most of us, most of the time. Our lives are tossed about relentlessly by the turbulence of the surface waves. How do we learn to sink just those crucial 'ten feet', into the stillness at the centre of ourselves? How might we encourage that deep inner relaxation which is the sign of surrender and openness to whatever God may wish to show us?

Preparing for prayer

Before you begin a time of this kind of relaxed prayerfulness, it is good to stop for a moment and remember what you are about to do. You are approaching God, the Lord of all creation, and asking him for the gift of prayer, through his Holy Spirit. You might find it helpful to use some personal way of marking this moment of humble petition. For example, I have a little pot of scented balm, which I use each day as a kind of 'anointing' on my forehead to remind myself that I am asking to come, in prayer, in to the presence of God. This in itself helps to steady me into stillness and reflectiveness. Another helpful way of marking the start of prayer is by lighting a candle and spending a few moments in its light.

There are many ways of relaxing, and you will no doubt have your own favourite method. There is no need to practise complicated techniques or go on any expensive courses! Relaxing is just what it says it is. Find a comfortable place, perhaps a reasonably firm chair. Sit upright, but not rigid, so that your back is straight and your feet are placed firmly on the floor. Rest your hands loosely in your lap or on your knees, whatever feels right for you. You may like to close your eyes, or, if this feels more natural for you, just focus your gaze on some object that will attract your wandering thoughts without distracting you, such as a candle, a flower, a picture or icon or a cross, or something that has personal meaning for you. For example, I have an open oyster shell, and a special stone that I sometimes use as a focus.

Entering sacred space

In Chapter 2 we looked at a way of discovering a 'sacred space' in your imagination by using your memory. Many people find this kind of memory a useful gateway into meditative prayer. I have one friend, for example, who often goes, in prayer, to a particular path in her imagination which leads to a park bench. She 'sits down' there and meets Jesus in her own way. Very often she has told me later of her trip to the bench that morning, and what it has revealed to her! Other people go to an imaginary room inside themselves, and close the door (as Jesus himself told us to do when we pray), so as to be alone in their meeting with the Lord.

Another friend, who lives with a boisterous family in the inner city has no space to call her own except the view from the window of her second storey flat. But from that window she can see a particular tree, which accompanies her prayer all through the year, from the cloudy white of blossom time, through all the greens of spring and summer and the yellows and browns of autumn, to the stark, bare winter branches. The tree is often her 'soul-friend' when she has no other.

Sacred space may also be discovered in our own experience and our own story. The Celts held certain significant places in creation to be especially sacred. These included wells, springs, boundaries of all kinds, bridges, doorways and causeways. When you reflect on your own life's journey, do you notice any times that have this kind of significance for you:

• Any times when you have felt yourself to be 'at the bottom of the well' but where, in fact, you have discovered living water that has given you a new lease of life?
• Any times when you have felt new energy springing up in you?
• Any times when you have felt you were walking the extremities of experience? Perhaps times of great suffering or intense joy?
• Any times when you have felt you were in transition between two phases of your life, as if crossing a bridge or a causeway towards an unknown future?
• Any times when you have felt you were standing in front of a closed

door, yet which, with hindsight you can see have become gateways to a time of new growth?

Some people find it helpful to take off their shoes on entering what they sense to be the sacred space in which they meet God in a special way.

Any of these may help you to enter into sacred space within yourself. Simply let the memory arise, unhampered, and ask God to consecrate it for you. Let it become the start point for your journey into prayer, and your descent to 'ten feet down'.

Your body – your ally

In all this talk of imagination and memory, we are in danger of forgetting that we are all embodied creatures, and that our physical being is as much a part of our prayer as our thoughts, feelings and memories.

There is one sacred space which is always there for you, wherever and however you live, and that is your own body. Your body can be your friend, your ally and your faithful collaborator in the great adventure of prayer, with just a little, gentle training. The body that feels so full of itches and aches, the brain that is only waiting for a chance to rush off to attend to the day's agenda, and the senses that want to wander off after every sound and smell can actually *help* you to enter prayer. Here are a few ways in which this can happen. You might like to try them out and use any one that appeals to you on a particular day:

- Try tensing all your muscles and then letting them go, one by one, becoming conscious of how each part of you is becoming relaxed and 'letting go'.

- Concentrate your attention on one part of your body – let's say, your little toe. Either stay with that one part for as long as you can, or, if you prefer, gradually move your attention round each part of your body in turn. Become aware of how each part is feeling, any discomfort or other sensation such as the pressure of your shoe, or of the chair against your back.

- Notice your own breathing. Become fully conscious of every breath, as you breathe in and as you breathe out. When you breathe out, let all your surface worries and pre-occupations go, one by one (think of them as you do this, and deliberately surrender them out of your control into

God's). When you breathe in, take into yourself the peace of God. Let the steady rhythm of your breathing calm you and bring you into a natural balance.

- Become aware of your own pulse or heartbeat. As you notice each beat of your heart, reflect that God is holding you in being through every second of your life, for 'in him we live and move and have our being'.

- Use a mantra, or a simple word or phrase that speaks to you in some way, to steady your mind into inner silence. Choose a word like 'Maranatha' – 'Come, Lord Jesus' – and repeat it over and over until it becomes almost like breathing. This is a way of occupying the upper levels of your mind and leaving the deeper reaches of yourself free to be present to the silence of prayer.

- Listen very attentively to the sounds around you. Begin with the noises in the outside world, the traffic, the birds, the neighbours. Then move your attention to your own room. Listen to the humming of the radiator, the gurgling of the pipes, the creaking of the wood. Finally, bring your attention right inside yourself and become aware of the sounds within you, especially your heartbeat.

And inner stillness can, paradoxically, often be found in action. Swimming is an excellent opportunity for prayer. If you enjoy swimming you may find that your half hour in the pool can become an oasis of prayer in itself. Let the water support you, and become aware of its buoyancy beneath you, just as God's love supports you. Notice the centre of gravity in yourself, moving steadily through the water, and realise that the whole exercise is one of balance. Far more important than the sometimes wild movements of your arms and legs is this deep inner centre of gravity, which holds you in harmony and in balance with the water. Of course you don't think about it when you are swimming, and neither are you conscious of this innermost balance when you pray, but this invisible pivot point is nevertheless the inner compass that governs your movement. The action of swimming can also act as a physical mantra, keeping your mental processes occupied with the one operation of swimming, and leaving the rest of you free to follow the call of prayer.

Steady walking can have the same effect, and is another way of expressing an inner desire to be directed towards God, and beyond yourself. You may find it helpful to use a verbal mantra along with your walking. For example, you could match the rhythm of your steps to a phrase like 'In you I live, and move, and have my being'.

And after prayer

When your prayer period comes to an end, it is helpful to close it with a familiar prayer, such as The Lord's Prayer, which also acts as a reminder that, though we pray individually, we are also praying, constantly, in community. As the hymn says 'The voice of prayer is never silent' as the earth spins. All who seek God are part of an unceasing circle of prayer, and as one person ends his prayer another is just beginning. The use of a prayer shared by all as a conclusion to your personal prayer reminds you of your place in the entire communion of faith.

Those who are familiar with Roman Catholic practices may also find the gesture of making a small sign of the cross on the forehead, the lips and the heart helpful. This is commonly done by individuals just before the Gospel is read during the Mass. Not being a 'cradle Catholic' myself, I have never established exactly what it is supposed to signify, but I have long since discovered my own meanings for it. I therefore use this gesture frequently at the end of a period of prayer and the start of a new day, to express my desire for God's blessing today 'on every thought in my head, every word on my lips and every stirring in my heart'. I add a fourth 'sign of the cross' to the back of my hand, to express the desire for a blessing on 'everything I write and every task I do today'.

However, I feel that it is important not to let such habits or gestures become automatic or mechanical, which could cause them to degenerate into superstitious practices. Let them come from your heart, if they come at all. Let them express what you really desire.

If you have been using a candle, when you blow it out watch, and smell, the smoke rise and disappear into the air. Your prayer will do that too. It will seem to have finished, and disappeared. But in reality it will have become part of the very air you breathe. It will have slipped silently, but fragrantly, into your life and into the life of all creation. It will have become a carrier of grace for the whole human family. You will go forward into your daily life carrying its power in your heart in very real, though invisible, ways, which I hope will become clearer to you as we move forward in this journey.

TAKING IT FURTHER ...

Imagine your desire for stillness, both inner and outer, as the coming to rest of a glass of muddy water. You might see this glass as the container of your consciousness. In its shaken, disturbed state, it is opaque, useless and even potentially harmful. But as you sink into prayer, watch the cloudiness sink with you.

Ever so gradually the water at the top of the glass becomes clear again, and the mud sinks deeper.

Notice, as you gaze, how the band of clear water widens, and the layer of mud narrows at the bottom of the glass, even as it settles and thickens in density.

Eventually the stilling, settling process is complete. The water in the glass is pure, giving you clarity of vision and wholesome water to quench your inner thirst (and perhaps to give to others who are thirsty).

And the mud? A place, perhaps, where God will plant the seed of something new. Both elements are part of his plan – our clarity and purity, and our mud. Only our own confusion clouds the issue.

Coming to stillness in prayer can feel a bit like beachcombing, walking slowly along the shoreline, simply noticing the movement of the waves and the brush of the breeze on your skin, and all the while alert to whatever treasure may have been left at your feet by the tide. A picture like this, brought to mind by a photograph given to me by a friend, helped me to find stillness for prayer during a bumpy motorway bus journey to work one morning. Perhaps I might share it with you . . ..

. . . This morning I am travelling to work on the bus, for the first time. A very different experience after the steady, familiar rhythm of the rails. Can I pray on the bus, I wonder? I can't pick up the rhythm of my breathing. It all gets submerged in the joggling and shaking as the bus slows and speeds and rounds corners and staggers across busy crossroads. And still the maker of heaven and earth can't be silenced by a bus on a congested motorway. Surely not.

I look at the seascape photograph a friend has given me and let myself

The tide of prayer flows
into the steady rock
of God's ever-presence.

be on the shoreline. It takes me to the beach and reminds me that there is sacred space at the meeting point. The waves break over the shore. Waves, light and restless and impermanent. Breaking. Waves of my lived reality, coming and going and throwing me about, and breaking. Those things that occupy almost all of my conscious being, almost all of the time, simply breaking and leaving just a shower of spray as a last image of themselves against a steady sky. The waves of my lived life, breaking against the bedrock of your truth. And that is prayer, and that is sacred space.

The waves of my prayer are gentle enough today in spite of the jumps and starts of motorway travel. They come to your shore humbly today. Just asking for a little space to land and do their breaking. But it isn't always like that. There are days when they heave themselves over to you like grey mountains, swelling and straining, heavy with pain and the unmanageable forces of their own energy.

And sometimes I hardly notice them, as they come lapping like tame kittens, searching for a little sustenance from the sandy beaches, spreading themselves ever so thinly, ever so far, into the flatness. They come under heavy grey skies, reflecting threat and fear. Or they sparkle when the sun shines, and scatter happiness like foam across the rocks. Or they creep in tears to seek your comfort and linger in your rock pools, begging for shelter until the tide turns.

These are my prayers, Lord. And yours is the rock and the solid beach and the steady shoreline. And I meet you in this sacred space. You receive me there, and I wander in my prayer like a beachcomber, mainly just for the joy of being there, but from time to time there will be gifts among the shingle, waiting to be discovered and gratefully gathered. A beautiful shell that reflects the colours of eternity. A persistent crab that raises a family in the rocks, against the odds, against the tide. A word from you, to change my world today.

My lived reality breaks daily against the rock that is you. It flings itself senselessly, instinctively against your cliffs, demanding and confronting, surging into the caverns of darkness, emptily echoing. And it ripples lovingly across the gentle welcoming sand, on its better days.

But the moment isn't for ever. The waters of our meeting are soon sucked out to sea again. Reluctantly withdrawing, whence they came. Yet not unchanged. Drawn back into the swell again, but never ever the same again. The tide of prayer ebbs again, and I am back on the high seas again. No longer who I was a prayer ago, nor yet who I will be another prayer away, beyond the next tide's turning. There is sadness in withdrawing, but there is strength in the power of the swell, and there is hope.

Prayer has happened. Your gift given and received, at the breaking point, when my tide spreads itself in a gesture of surrender and my waves collapse, exhausted, on the shore. Prayer happens when I break into the spray on the bedrock of your reality. And then the moment is over. I open my eyes, and the trees are breaking into blossom on the dual carriageway, casting their own traces of dappled springtime spray across the oceans of a grey-blue sky above them.

And there is a long day ahead, until my tide can flow again onto your waiting beaches. And the rock remains, and the beaches. Only the tide moves in and out.

For a very readable guide to these and other forms of relaxation into prayer, the book *Sadhana – A Way to God* by Anthony de Mello (Doubleday Image, 1978) may also be helpful.

4. REFLECTING, CONNECTING

The bridge between prayer and daily life

'My time of prayer this morning was very peaceful, very healing, but I can't actually remember a thing about it . . . .'

Does this kind of comment ring any bells with you? For 'my time of prayer', you could read 'my day of recollection' or even 'my retreat'. The problem is familiar to many of us. Prayer seems, sometimes, to go in one ear and out the other. We know that it was 'a good thing', but we don't really begin to understand why, or what effect it may have had on us. Over the years I have heard so many people lament the fact that the time they have given over to meditation and stillness has seemed to flow on, like a river, leaving no apparent trace of itself behind in their lives. This experience can, sadly, easily seduce us into giving up on prayer, or letting it lapse into mere daydreaming.

We are, of course, seriously missing the point when we look for 'results' from our prayer. As long as we are expecting some kind of 'payback', the focus will remain firmly on ourselves and our hopes and expectations, and not on God. We will be concentrating, as Teresa of Avila puts it, on 'the consolations of God', rather than on 'the God of consolations'. Nevertheless, prayer, if it is authentic, *will* make a difference to us, to our lives, to our way of making decisions and of being human in the surroundings in which we find ourselves. But that difference may only become apparent to us over time, and as a result of patient observation – simply noticing God's action in our lives and the ways in which he may be encouraging, warning, challenging us. We will notice these things not so much during prayer itself, when our focus will be on God just for his own sake, but in the time *after* prayer when we stop to reflect on what seems to have been happening during the prayer.

There are two practices that can help in this process, and change what could become merely a pious ritual of 'saying our prayers' or even 'doing our meditation', into an authentic and life-giving encounter with our deepest selves in God.

- We can form the habit of reflecting, *after* prayer and in our minds, on what has been happening *during* prayer, in our hearts.
- We can begin to make real and grounded connections between our prayer and our lived experience, and between the story of God's self-expression, particularly in Scripture, and the mystery of his self-expression in our own lives and personalities.

Cut and dried?

A farmer friend told me, one day, that according to an old tradition, the cut corn at harvest time was supposed to lie in the fields to dry until the church bells had rung across it three times – that is, three Sundays.

In the dubious weather conditions with which our islands are blessed, this might sound like a vain hope, but as my friend gave me this piece of wisdom the words that came to my mind were 'cut and dried'. It made me wonder about my own ways of discerning things and making decisions. Mostly, I realised, my decisions and so-called discernments get cut and gathered on the same day, with no time for maturing, so sure am I of my own defective judgements!

But the habit of reflection can make a difference to this unseemly haste. It can slow us down just long enough to make a short space of time after prayer 'for the corn to dry', before we rush off to meet the demands of daily life. It provides an opportunity just to let our own feelings about our prayer time come to the surface – a chance to stand back and notice how the time has been, gathering any fruits of that time that seem especially to come to mind. It may be all we need to ensure that the corn of our prayer is not only cut but dried as well, so that it has time and space to mature and become more fully a part of our lives.

The practice of reflection

You may well be wondering how, having carved out some time for prayer, you are supposed to find any extra time on top of that to do your 'reflecting'. Well, it really needn't become a burden. Ideally, if you can find the extra five or ten minutes, bring your time of prayer to a close and then make a deliberate break, perhaps by moving to a different place, or making yourself a cup of coffee, and then settle for just a few minutes and notice:

How did you go into the time of prayer? What issues were in your mind? How were you feeling? Tired, fresh, energetic or unwell? How long did you intend to give to prayer? How did you focus your prayer – on a passage of Scripture, for example? What particular 'grace' were you asking for or desiring?

How were your feelings during the time of prayer? How was the time for you – comfortable, uncomfortable, short or long, tedious or interesting, turbulent or peaceful? Did you notice any movements of mood or feeling during the prayer time. Did anything in the prayer trigger feelings of elation, despondency, hope, anxiety? Were you able to express these feelings to God and to yourself?

How do you feel now, looking back over the time of prayer?

- Did you spend the time in prayer that you originally intended to spend? The experience of many praying people is that it isn't so important to pray for a particular length of time, but rather to stay *faithful* to whatever time you have decided to set aside. Try to resist the temptation to cut short the period you have decided upon. Prayer often 'comes alive' at the very end of the time you have given to it.
- Do you feel you have received the 'grace' you were asking for? (Keep an open mind about this last question – sometimes the 'grace you asked for' can come in ways and at times when you least expect it, often as you go on with your normal daily life, but it is nevertheless good to remind yourself, in reflection, what you were actually seeking in your prayer.)
- Is there anything in the time of prayer that draws you back, anything you feel you would like to return to next time? Any 'unfinished business'?
- Is there anything in your prayer that you especially want to store in your memory? Did anything (for example in Scripture) connect to where you feel you are in your lived experience?

And if this 'ideal' situation, of ten minutes' quiet reflection over a cup of coffee, simply doesn't exist in your day, this needn't become a problem. Everything we are exploring in this journey into prayer is going to be discovered in our daily lives, just as they are, just as we are living them. The kitchen, the computer workstation, the coffee shop – these are our cloisters and this is where we will find the God of all things. Your reflection can be woven into your day and picked up again and again, whenever there is a free minute. Just let the awareness of your time with God float at the edges of your consciousness, so that it can surface whenever there is a relevant prompt. You may find, for example, that things happen, or are said, during the day, that bring to life something that arose in your prayer. These things may go a long way towards deepening your prayer experience, giving it real meaning in your life and helping you to notice how the grace you are desiring is being given, gift-wrapped in God's surprises.

You might find it helpful to make a short note of anything that strikes you, arising out of your reflection. This is particularly important if you are sharing your journey with a 'soul-friend' (see Chapter 23). Keeping a little notebook of your reflection thoughts can help to focus later conversations with a companion. It can also help you to see how your journey with God has been moving through the weeks and months and years, how issues have been resolved over time, how you have grown in faith and hope and love. In this way the corn continues to ripen as it lies in the field waiting for the threefold chimes of the church bells.

Connecting and re-connecting – crossing the causeway

One of the most precious graces of the process of reflection is that it gives us the space in which to notice, and take into ourselves, the ways in which prayer is connecting with our lived reality.

To help explore this process of connection, and since we are at the beginning of an 'adventure into prayer', we might do worse than go, in our imagination, to a place that was in so many ways a cradle of prayer in these islands of Britain. If you were to follow in the steps of St Aidan and St Cuthbert (both of them saintly, unassuming Celtic monks, who, in the seventh century AD, brought the Gospel from Scotland to the north of England), you would find yourself on a small tidal island in the North Sea, just off the coast of Northumberland. To get to this island, the Holy Island of Lindisfarne, you would have to wait for low tide, in order to cross the sands by means of the causeway, which is accessible for only a few hours between the tides.

A causeway is revered as an especially sacred place in the Celtic mind and heart. It is a place of transition, a means of passing from where you are to where you desire to be. In this sense, you might, with truth, call a cause-way a channel of grace. But it is also a powerful parable of prayer. Still in your imagination, let the tide ebb, and then walk quietly across the

Let the tide ebb,
and walk quietly across
the causeway.

causeway, as if you were walking into the sacred space of silence and prayer. Is there anything specific, any issue in your life, that you are carrying with you today from the mainland to the island? If so, simply let it be there, without any deliberate effort to 'resolve' it. Allow the stillness of the holy place to receive you, welcome you, enfold you. And as you sink into the stillness, allow the tide to come in and encircle you in your island-space. Slowly the causeway disappears, submerged by the rising tides. You are alone with God on the island of your prayer.

Eventually the tide turns. Your time of prayer is over. The water recedes. The causeway begins to reappear. It is time for the return journey, back to the mainland. Perhaps you are eager to return, relieved that the time of prayer has passed, if it has been difficult or dry. Perhaps you are reluctant to return, wishing that the island-time could last for ever. Either way the mainland beckons you. It is time to *re-connect* to the place of your lived life.

What do you carry with you as you return to the mainland of your life? Will your memory of the island-time be washed away with the incoming tide, like footprints on the sands? Or is there something you would like to gather and garner, as food for the onward journey? What happened on the island that will change the way you make choices and relationships on the mainland?

Living the fifth gospel

The picture of the island, connected to the mainland by its causeway, can help to open up a different kind of 'way' in our hearts, submerged as they are, for so much of the time, beneath the floods of life. Prayer, and the reflection that follows it, can begin to reveal our own personal Gospel story – each individual pilgrim's 'fifth gospel'. The process of *connecting* our time with God in prayer with our time with God and all his people in his living world can help us to take Gospel values, very specifically, into our own way of living out our days and responding to his call to become his sons and daughters. Perhaps an example may help to show how this can work . . ..

I have a friend whose life can truly be called a minefield. She has ex-perienced far more than her fair share of hardship and heartbreak, yet she is a person whom I would describe as 'translucent'. The light of her spirit seems to shine out of her, unhindered. One morning, after I had seen this friend, the daily reading was the story of how Jesus sent his disciples off in a boat across the sea of Galilee 'when the winds were against them', and how he came walking across the water to them just as they thought they were about to go under. As I let this Gospel story form my prayer, my friend came to mind. The picture that presented itself in my imagination was of a lighthouse, steadily beaming out its promise of courage and hope, while surrounded by tempestuous seas. My friend was such a lighthouse, I began to realise.

But it was afterwards, in my time of reflection on the prayer, that the connections came to life. Translucency, like my friend's, I noticed, often seems to occur in people whom life appears in some way to have 'broken'.

And lighthouses are constructed out to sea on the most dangerous rocks or sand-banks. My thoughts turned to my own life, and a particular reluctance to risk a very specific rocky hazard in my life's seas, even though I know that a lighthouse planted safely inland in a sheltered grove is no use at all! I was led to reflect on the cost, in terms of risk and of loneliness, of being 'a lighthouse' and challenged to ask myself whether I was prepared to pay such a price in my own circumstances.

In this example, the process of *reflection* helped me to notice the ways in which God was moving through my feelings and my memories through this particular time of prayer, and to recognise the places where he was stirring up my attention and challenging my response. And the process of *connection* gave me some real, solid guidelines on how to take this truth into my lived experience and make it incarnate, perhaps in a new way of being present to an old difficulty.

TAKING IT FURTHER . . .

It is common, in human experience, to find that when our attention is focused on something specific, we will become aware of that 'something' far more often than would normally be the case. For example, if you are waiting for a lift with someone who drives a red car, you will be amazed at how many red cars there are on the roads! We have a large spruce tree in our front garden, and I often used to tell people about it as a landmark to look out for if they were trying to find our home for the first time . . . until one disgruntled visitor told me just how many spruce trees he had counted in other people's front gardens, before locating ours!

But we can make use of this human tendency as an aid in reflecting on our prayer. Try remembering just one important thing about your prayer and carrying it through the day with you. It may be the fact that you were feeling unexpectedly elated, or dejected, by something that arose in prayer, or it may be a particular connection you noticed between something in Scripture and something in your own life. Just carry it with you, whatever it is, and notice any moments during the day when the same kind of thing comes into your awareness again. The same kind of feeling, perhaps, or the same connection. Each time this happens, allow it to deepen your prayer, as an artist might add touches of colour and shading, bit by bit, to a picture he has begun.

Make friends with your 'causeway'. Gradually let yourself become familiar with the feeling of moving backwards and forwards between the 'island' of your prayer and the 'mainland' of your daily life. Begin to notice the rhythm of your own 'tides', and the natural interactions between 'high tide', when you are alone with God on the island, and 'low tide' when you are wholly engaged with the demands and strains of life in your personal circumstances. Notice, and perhaps make a written note of, any issues you are carrying from the mainland to the island, and any gifts you are taking back from the island to the mainland. Are these gifts for yourself, do you think, or for other people as well? Welcome this 'trade route' in your heart, and let it become fruitful. Become more aware of what you are hoping for from it, and how these hopes are being fulfilled.

5. WHAT ARE YOU LOOKING FOR?

Focusing on what we really desire

Two men, former disciples of John the Baptist, just introduced to Jesus, turn to follow him and are stopped in their tracks when Jesus turns round to face them, looks straight into their eyes, and asks them this question. (John 1:35–9).

If you can imagine yourself in their position, how do you feel when the Lord holds your gaze and asks you what you are really looking for, in your following of him. His eyes seem to search out your innermost desires. Dare you do the same?

The disciples are thrown by the question. Perhaps they cast around in their minds for some appropriate answer. What comes out is just another question: 'Where do you live, Rabbi?' To which he invites them into a life-changing journey: 'Come and see!'

Like the disciples, each of us, too, has, in our own way, made the first tentative steps to follow the one who beckons. We know a little of where we are coming from, but nothing of where we are going to. Perhaps we hesitate, reluctant to take the next step into the beyond without some assurance that our leader, at least, has a map. He offers us no such assurance. Quite the reverse. He turns instead and places the unanswered question back in our own hearts.

What are you looking for?

Asking for what you desire

We are not the first pilgrims to be disconcerted by this question. Through the centuries many believers have discovered for themselves that one of the most difficult steps in prayer is to notice what it is that you are really seeking, and then, quite simply, to ask God for it. In some traditions this is called 'asking for the grace'. All it means is noticing where your own desire, in this particular prayer, is *focused*, and naming that desire to God in your prayer.

It all sounds very simple, in theory. In practice it can look quite different. I remember the first time that I was faced with the question myself. I was making my first retreat, and on the first morning my retreat guide asked me exactly that: 'What grace are you seeking in your prayer today?' And I was as floored as those first disciples must have been! It had never occurred to me to ask God for what I wanted, and I realised that I really didn't have any clear idea myself about what I wanted, or hoped for, from the day's prayer. And, frankly, at the time, I couldn't see why it should be so important. Surely I could safely leave it all with God, who, after all, knew far better than I did, what I wanted and what I needed.

But, of course, the exercise is not at all about informing God of our needs and desires, but, much more necessarily, bringing these needs and desires up from our own unconscious depths into the realms of consciousness so that we ourselves become aware of them. When we 'ask for what we desire' we are actually pinpointing the real flashpoints of our own desiring.

Two questions arise immediately:

- Why do our own desires matter so much?
- Why are we sometimes so reluctant to express them?

Divine discontent

When asked: 'What do you desire?', people's reactions vary enormously. Some will deny that they have any desires at all, because they believe that as Christians they should be content with whatever life gives. Others find that there are so many desires milling around in their hearts that they don't know where to begin.

And perhaps almost all of us have an uneasy feeling about our desires, and have grown up feeling that we should be suppressing our own desires in an attempt, rather, to seek 'God's Will'. Most of us have been strongly influenced by a sense of our desires as being somehow 'a bad thing', or at the very least, untrustworthy and likely to seduce us into error. While 'God's Will' (whatever that is) can be trusted – if only it were not so unhelpfully invisible!

The very word 'desire' carries connotations of sin. The word 'will' on the other hand, seems to carry weight and authority, however oppressive. The programming goes deep into our hearts and minds that if we are enjoying something, it must be wrong, and that an iron will, reflected in an iron face, is more likely to be morally acceptable.

Yet God, we believe, *desires* us into being. He *desires* our wholeness so much that he allows himself to be broken for its sake. He awakens our desire for him by pouring his own Spirit through our lives. Our hearts *long for* him, we say, just as a river seeks its ocean homing. The whole of creation lives and grows under the impulse of desire. Every new life springs from a moment of desire. Every flower is pollinated by attraction and desire. Every step of discovery is made out of a desire to go beyond – always beyond the horizon of the known. Every meal we eat, the very sustenance of our living, is taken because our bodies express their need of food in the desire that we call appetite. It is, perhaps, no mere cliché, after all, to affirm that it is love (expressed as desire) that makes the world go round.

Why, then, do we feel the need to *suppress* our own desires? Might it not be possible that our deepest desires indeed flow in the same eternal stream as God's desire for us and for all his creation? If this were so, then the apparently incurable discontent we experience, when our desires remain unfulfilled, could be a divine, as well as a human discontent.

Can discontent be divine? Perhaps it depends on whether that discontent is focused on our *deepest* desires or if it has settled more superficially on our *lesser* wants and wishes. I am discontented when it rains on my day off or when the postman doesn't bring the letter I was hoping for. This is little more than petulance. I am discontented when an important relationship goes wrong. This is disappointment and regret. But divine discontent seems to be something quite different – something positive even. It is what spurs me on to make the very best use of the gifts I have, or to go to extreme lengths to be close to someone who needs me. We see the evidence of divine discontent all around us: it is what makes the chick hatch and what fires the soul of the concert pianist. It is what leads us to realise, with St Augustine, that 'our soul finds no rest until it finds its rest in God.'

Beyond the lottery

One very important reason for the apparent mismatch between our desires and God's Desire lies in the fact that we so easily get side-tracked, by many lesser wants and wishes, from our search for what we *most deeply* desire. We can name what we think we want, but it is much harder to probe beneath it and discern what lies at the roots of that 'wanting'.

I experienced these layers of 'wanting' once during a conversation with a friend on the train on the way to work. We began by exchanging light-hearted comments: 'Are you still here then? Not redundant yet? Not won the lottery?' It was Monday morning, and my friend smiled ruefully and told me that on the previous Friday she had only just missed winning the 'Spot the Ball' competition in her local newspaper. She bewailed the fact that she had won just £5, and so narrowly missed winning £200,000.

Now that is bad luck! I commiserated with her. Then, more out of idle curiosity than anything else, I asked her what she would have done with the £200,000 if she had won it. At that point there was a noticeable change in the nature of the conversation. The banter was set aside and she became quite thoughtful. We sat for a moment in silence. Then she told me that she would have bought a house with the prize money. I let her continue with her musings. A few more moments and she revealed that she would have bought a big house with a garden, in Birmingham. She was obviously imagining this dream home even as she spoke. Then came the crunch, in just a few words that came straight from her heart: 'I'd take my mother back there to her roots, to a nice home in the place where she grew up, the only place where she really longs to be!'

Perhaps you can see, in this example, how deep the question 'What are you looking for?' can go. For my friend, it could have been answered at several different levels: 'I want to win a lot of money', 'I want a big house', 'I want to live in Birmingham', but underneath all of these, and much more muted, were longings that she hadn't realised herself that she had: 'I want to make my mother happy before she dies,' and 'We are longing to go back to our roots.' I don't know whether she thought any more about this conversation, but if she did, she might have begun to understand something of how our deepest desires affect and drive us. Even the desire to win the lottery, though it can be dismissed as a materialistic whim, is often the tip of a hidden iceberg of desire. What does that iceberg contain? It is well worth doing a little deep-sea diving to find out, and prayer gives us the perfect place to do just that. The exercises at the end of this chapter suggest ways of investigating both our long-term and our more immediate desires in prayer.

Too hot to handle?

Another common reason why we hesitate to express the deepest desires of our hearts, even in the silence and secrecy of prayer, is because we think they are desires we ought not to have. Perhaps what we desire is something quite illicit. Maybe we *do* covet our neighbour's ox and ass and husband! Maybe we *do* wish our boss would meet with a fatal accident! To 'desire' such things is by no means the same as bringing them about! Feelings are neutral – neither morally right or wrong in themselves. It is what we *do* about those feelings, how we turn them into action, that makes them morally loaded. Which isn't to say that such extreme feelings can easily be expressed, even to our closest friends.

There is, however, no reason at all why they may not be expressed to God in our prayer (which is also a way of expressing them to ourselves, and acknowledging their existence and their power in honest humility). Or is there? Perhaps we cannot express them, even in our prayer, because our image of God is punitive. Is he the judge, the policeman, the angry father or avenging lover, waiting to find a chink in our armour? If you do find that you hit a block when trying to express such deep, and possibly painful desires in prayer, you may find it helpful to ask yourself what images you have of God, and whether these images are helping you to draw closer to him, or, rather, keeping you at a distance from him. And remember that when you do express such desires to God, you are not asking him to fulfil them, but you are simply bringing yourself to him, just as you are, and opening up your innermost feelings in his presence. You can safely leave it to him to guide you through your inner minefields in ways that will strengthen your trust in him and in yourself, and release the positive energy that is locked up in your desires.

Claiming the energy

Yes, there *is* energy locked up in our desires. Just as electric power flows from the negative to the positive poles, so too there is a flow of energy that seems to flow between where we are and where we desire to be. That gap, between our desires and their fulfilment, is, truly, a creative gap. Feelings of love, for example, generate the power to do things we never imagined we could ever do. Feelings of compassion can produce stamina and fortitude

to go to extreme lengths for another person. And feelings of anger can produce the energy and courage to confront and oppose situations that are
harming ourselves or others.

This energy is ours for the claiming. And we can claim it by facing our
own deepest longings and desires (whether they appear to be 'good' or
'bad') with trust and integrity. When we make a practice, in our prayer (and
at other times) of noticing, and naming, what we really want, what we are
really looking for, we are gradually learning to recognise our deepest desire
and to discover that the stream of our longings is the same stream of God's
longing for *us*.

So it becomes a valid, indeed a crucial question in prayer: what am I
really asking for? Am I asking God to attend to my petulant complaints and
arrange the world, and its climate, around my wishes? Am I asking him to
wave a magic wand over my life's disappointments and regrets? Or am I
asking him to enter the deepest layers of my personality, and grow me into
the person I really am, the person he has created me to become? If this
third option is our choice, we will surely experience divine discontent in
all our moments until God's dream of us is fulfilled, but all the while our
own desiring will be moving closer towards complete harmony with *his*
Desire for *us*. Our will and his will be one. The only difference is one of
scale. Our own desiring encompasses just our own whole-making, and
perhaps that of those immediately around us. God's Desire, God's Will,
encompasses the wholeness of all his creation, and he will not cease from
his own divine discontent until, as a Buddhist guru once expressed it, 'the
last blade of grass is redeemed'.

St John's Gospel ends with a similar question as the one with which it
begins. This time the question is addressed by the risen Jesus to Mary of
Magdala (John 20:14). Those first disciples in Chapter 1 had been just setting out on their quest for the Lord. Mary thinks she has come to the end.
The disciples had just discovered Jesus. Mary has just lost him. They still
had everything before them. She feels that there is nothing but grief and
emptiness ahead of her. And into this terrible emptiness, Jesus speaks his
question again: 'Who are you looking for?'

And this, I believe, is also the pattern of *our* desiring. We begin with our
many 'whats'. Our little wants and wishes, our bigger hopes and dreams,
our deep, and sometimes hidden, desires. And we go down and down,
deeper into their roots. We follow Jesus' invitation to 'come and see', to

find out who we really are and what 'makes us tick'. And at the end of our searching we come to the place where, it seems, we first began, but knowing now that it is no longer the 'what' but the 'whom' we are looking for. Knowing that all our desires are drawing us towards the deepest desire of all, to be truly and fully ourselves and to be one with God and with each other.

TAKING IT FURTHER ...

I was on holiday one summer in the Spanish Pyrenees. It wasn't easy to find a place to stay, but eventually we found a room for a few nights, in a small village at the edge of a spectacular National Park. It was an ideal spot, except for the fact that there was a hydro-electric power station outside the window, and the days and nights were alive with the throbbing of its generators.

We spent a few marvellous days exploring the wild mountainous tracts of the National Park. Most of all I remember the joy of finding a tiny mountain stream, which began as a spring high among the peaks, and the adventure of trying to follow its course, right down to the valley. Sometimes it would show itself in little rushes of clear water, or cool, bright pools, reflecting the brilliance of the skies and giving life to a carpet of mountain flowers. Then it would disappear, leaving only the slightest hint of a river that had gone underground and now rolled on unseen. And again it would re-appear, perhaps as a little waterfall, or a more dignified channel of deepening water. Then it would be gone again, perhaps for miles, leaving us guessing as to which direction it might possibly have chosen. It felt as thought that stream was playing games with us. Now you see it, now you don't. It had a life and an energy all its own – sometimes so gentle, like a kitten, sometimes majestic. It was only as I lay in bed at night, listening to the rumble of the generators, that I realised that the playful, hideaway stream held in its elusive waters the power to bring heat and light and energy to an entire human community.

I share this story with you because it was a powerful picture for me of the stream of my desiring.

Playful springs and elusive streams
supply the power for
an entire community.

Perhaps you can name some of your own deep desires that find expression in its waters:

- Do you see any desires that bubble up in your life, obvious and visible, perhaps delighting you with their promise and their hope.
- Do you see any that frighten you by appearing as precipitous waterfalls that could throw you onto dangerous rocks.
- Do you have any sense of desires that remain stubbornly out of sight, refusing to be acknowledged.
- Can you name any *particular* desires that you hold in your heart that come into any of these categories? Be specific: not just 'I want to fulfil

my potential', but 'I want to study astro-physics and get a job on the European Space Programme.'

Now, in your imagination, go down to the village at the foot of the mountain. Listen to the throb of the generators. Notice each house, lit and warmed by electricity. And let yourself simply become aware of that unbroken stream of your own deep desire, which is energising your life in the same way.

Read cold, on a printed page, this suggestion may sound implausible. I can only urge you to *try* getting in touch with your own deep desires, because this is the only way to prove to yourself – by experiment – what energy they are releasing in your life.

To notice your more immediate desires, try starting each day with just a few moments' reflection on what you are hoping for in the coming 24 hours. Again, be specific. And try delving down a little to the real roots of these desires.

Once you feel more comfortable with this habit of focusing on what you are hoping for day by day, try applying the same technique when you begin a period of prayer. What hopes and wishes are you bringing to the prayer? Imagine Jesus sitting with you in your 'sacred space', asking you (very gently and lovingly) 'What are you looking for, *today*? What would you like me to do for you?'

Suppose you were to win a large sum of money (let's say half a million pounds), what would you do with it? What do your reflections on this question show you about where your deeper desires lie?

If you were told tomorrow that you only have three months left to live, how would you spend that time?

For more help in identifying the actual desires in your heart, where they have their roots, how the many conflicts between them are resolved, and the whole subject of the relationship between our desires and God's Will, see *Landmarks* by Margaret Silf (Darton, Longman and Todd, 1998).

Other books that you may find helpful in reflecting on your desires in prayer include:

What Do I Want in Prayer? by William A. Barry SJ (Paulist Press, 1994)

Befriending Our Desires by Philip Sheldrake SJ (Darton, Longman and Todd, 1994)

PART TWO
FOCUSING THE TELESCOPE

In the first section we laid two foundation stones for a life of personal prayerfulness. The first was the habit of cultivating inner stillness and allowing ourselves to sink 'ten feet down' to a state in which our hearts are ready to 'receive' and become aware of the ever-presence of God. The second was the need for reflection and review, to notice the real and specific ways in which our prayer connects to our daily lived experience, and to notice the movements of our own deep desires.

Once this inner stillness has been reached, and the practice of reflection has been established, we can begin to 'focus the telescope' of our prayer in particular ways. There are as many ways of doing this as there are people who are seeking God in prayer. No way is 'right' or 'wrong'. This section suggests just a few of the ways you might like to try.

6. The flat above the shop
Exploring our inner space

7. Your history, your mystery
Praying our stories

8. Action Replay
Reviewing the day with God

9. With love and prayers...
The prayer of intercession

10. Two column inches
Bringing the world's events to God

11. A quiver full of arrows
The habit of instant prayer

12. Zooming in
Going deeper, in the prayer of repetition

6. THE FLAT ABOVE THE SHOP

Exploring our inner space

'Who do you think you are?' The words might sound aggressive, but discovering the answer to the question, bit by bit, day by day, is the most thrilling and rewarding project you will ever engage in ....

There is a little shop on the A34 near Newcastle-under-Lyme. It sells electrical goods, and every time we go there I find myself fascinated by this place, because it gives me a clue for the search for 'who I am'. I think the reason for my fascination is that the shop is the ground floor of a three-storey house, like the one in the picture. The shop has a big display window, showing the goods it has for sale and the special offers, price lists, opening times and so on. The name above the shop tells you what the shop is there for. It doesn't tell you anything about the shopkeeper.

Above the shop is the floor where the family live. Its windows are smaller, and covered with net curtains. This is the private place for the family, still open to the world outside, but much more shielded, and certainly not 'open all hours'. You might go in there, and feel quite at ease, but only if you knew the family, or were invited there as a friend.

Then, right at the top of the house is the gable space, a third storey high above the main road. This is probably a small bedroom or a study or a child's den. The window is tiny. The person in the room can look out of it, but no one can look in, so it doesn't need elaborate curtains. You could look down onto the road from this window, but, up there in the third storey, your eyes would be much more likely to look upwards, because it is halfway to heaven up there! And what fascinates me especially about this top storey is that there are two initials engraved above the window, just below the roof. Presumably these are the initials of the first owner, but to the casual passer-by they must always remain a mystery

Why does this place intrigue me so much? Well, I think it is because it reminds me of the 'house' of my own life. I also have three 'storeys'. There is a the ground floor me, where I do my job and join my clubs and align myself with this or that good cause or interest group. My 'shop' part only

Climb the stairway up to
your own little garret.

shows my public self, and it opens up to the public for as long and as often
as I think necessary to keep the bread on my table and remain a reasonably social individual. You can look in my 'shop window' and deduce quite
a bit about the kind of person I am and how I am different from other

people, just as you can easily tell the difference between a butcher's and a baker's shop. But, at the end of the day, you still won't know much about the real me.

But if you could go upstairs, to the second storey, you would discover a lot more clues. Like: who my friends are, and what family I have; what colours I like; what books I read, and whether you feel at ease with me or not.

And, were you to be invited right up to the top of my house, you might glimpse something of the innermost reality of me that only God can fully know. That is where my initials are stamped – the name that he will give me for eternity, and that is a mystery to myself, as well as to you.

Of course, the house is only a metaphor, but if it appeals to you, you might like to think about your own 'house', and maybe even draw a picture of it. What is in your shop window? What is your public self about? How are your 'opening hours'? Are you on demand to your public too much? Or too little? Are they draining you, or enriching you? Do you think your 'shop' is doing well, or are you feeling close to bankruptcy? Do you ever wish your 'shop' were in some different trade? These are just a few fairly light-hearted questions to encourage you to notice the 'ground floor' of your life and how you feel about it.

Now go upstairs and explore your 'living quarters'. How are things up there? How is the family? Is the room lonely, or packed with friends. What do you find there about yourself and your preferences and interests? How easy do you feel about sharing this part of your 'house'? Is there anyone you feel you need to exclude from it, or anyone you long to invite in but feel you can't?

And finally, climb the winding staircase up to your little garret. How would you describe this innermost, secret space inside yourself? Does it feel peaceful, or turbulent right now? Look around this room, in your imagination. When you reflect on what it contains, would you feel easy about inviting a close friend into it or not? Is there anything you would want to put away in a cupboard first? Do you share this room, ever, with another human being? In your imagination, how does the atmosphere feel in this room: warm, accepting, welcoming, reproachful, frightening, imprisoning or liberating, suffocating or life-giving?

The walled garden

Maybe houses are not for you, but you see your inner world more like a garden? A favourite place of mine is an island off the north east coast of Britain. The first thing you would notice, if you landed on this, or any other island, would be the harbour and the beaches fringing the island's coastline. If you had the time to explore it more deeply, you would find the fields and forests further inland, where the islanders grow their crops and cultivate their trees and keep their animals. On my particular island, however, there is also a small, but very lovely castle, and close to the castle is a tiny walled garden, which is only accessible at certain times, when the gardener is in attendance. This garden is lovingly tended, and it blooms with a whole variety of herbs and blossoms. It was originally planted by the owners of the castle, who wanted it to be a special place which would express their own personal delight in life and also be a place where they could find peace and solitude to be themselves, away from their 'public' image.

I find a parable of my own inner spaces here on this island. I find aspects of myself that I might call the harbours and landing stages of my life within the human family. These are places where I meet people and let them into my life — or keep them out! I find a whole outer fringe of me — my beaches, where I am in direct contact, minute by minute, with the turbulent, demanding, unpredictable world around me. Then I move 'inland', where I can discover the 'what' and the 'how' of my existence. What is my work about? What 'crops' am I growing? What is my contribution to the day-to-day living of the human race? What am I best at? What am I bad at? Where are the wild, overgrown areas of my life, and where are my fields in better order? In what part of my 'island' do I feel most at home and comfortable? Where do I feel threatened?

And then we come to the walled garden. This is like the top storey of the house. It is my innermost space where I meet with God, and to which only a few other human hearts have access. What grows in that garden? God has planted it for his own delight, and for mine, and ultimately for the delight of all who dwell in his Kingdom. When I spend time in that walled garden, I am being invited to discover just who *God* thinks I am!

Another garden that always refreshes and inspires me is one that nestles in the heart of Chester Cathedral. This cathedral image, if it isn't too overwhelming, can also be a route to the heart of ourselves. It stands, visible and obvious in the High Street. Like us, it is physically there, present to the world around it. When we go inside we find a vast public space, open alike to tourists and worshippers. And our inner space too is partially open in this way to all those with whom we interact. To go deeper inside the cathedral, at Chester at least, you have to take a little trouble to find your way into the cloisters. This is a more private, prayerful place to be, like the inner reaches of ourselves, less frequented, more meaningful and reflective. There it is possible to walk round quietly, to circle the centre of ourselves, to be closer to the heartbeat that holds us in being. And as you walk round the cloisters, you will notice a little wooden door with a latch. Sometimes it is locked. But if you are lucky, and the door opens for you, you will find yourself on the threshold of a small, secluded garden, with a fountain at its centre. Here is the secret space of your meeting point with God, and it is fed by the spring of living water that God is opening up in your own heart.

Growing where you are planted

'If only I could have my life again, be born into a different family, choose a different job, a different lifestyle, begin again, knowing what I know now . . . .'

This is a day-dream in which almost everyone indulges from time to time. When I feel these thoughts coming on I find that a short while in my innermost garden helps me see things rather differently. For instance, I find that the spring bulbs can tell me their story. From them I hear an echo of the feelings I often have myself, of being buried beneath a suffocating weight of the clay of unwelcome circumstances, cold, wet, dark and alone. Then I hear their cry of startled discovery that this same deadening clay has been the provider of their nutrition all through the secret growing months. The circumstances we so often long to escape are the very place, and the *only* place that can provide the means of our growth and bring us to the moment of rebirth in the springtime.

And next time you have a chance to do so, try holding a seed in your hand – any seed will do. If you drop that seed into the ground it will, in its own good time, become whatever it is destined to be. When that time comes you might like to reflect on a simple equation:

The seed plus the soil equals the flower.

The soil – that cloying weight of unchangeable circumstances in which you live out your life – is the only added ingredient that turns the seed into the flower. In fact the flower is *made* of that soil. The loveliest, most fragrant blossom at the flower show is made of soil! But that soil has been transfigured and transformed by the hidden reality of the seed that is doing its silent becoming down in the depths of the earth. Small wonder that Jesus invited us to 'consider the lilies of the field'. They have a key to wisdom which we, perhaps, lost, when we first left the Garden.

TAKING IT FURTHER ...

A helpful exercise might be to invite God, in your prayer, to come with you into your 'house', and just to show him round, starting at the ground floor, and working up. When you have finished your tour, change roles with God for a few minutes, and ask *him* to guide *you* round, starting at the top, where you and he are closest, and working down to street level, and to show you how what happens in the garret filters its way down through the family quarters, to the shop, and out into the street.

In your imagination, take a boat out to your 'island' and spend some time exploring it. Explore its beaches and its jetties, then go inland and see what is growing there and what your island is all about. Finally, ask God to unlock the gate to your walled garden and take you inside. Ask him to introduce you to the flowers and shrubs and herbs that are growing there, to tell you how much he enjoys planting and tending them, and all that he hopes they will become. Simply share in his delight. Let this sanctuary of joy become a place to return to when you are struggling with all the problems in the surrounding fields.

If you can imagine yourself as a seed, or a spring bulb, buried deep in the winter earth, try becoming aware of the nature of the soil in which you are planted – the soil of your personal circumstances. How does this 'soil'

feel on the whole? Light, heavy, supportive, oppressive, nourishing or draining? Just reflect on it for a few minutes and see what descriptions come to mind. These are your real feelings about your circumstances, coming to the surface of your mind to claim your attention. Don't suppress them or judge them. They are pointers to your deepest self.

Now look back over the years of your life. Let it be springtime in your heart ... your seed or bulb has broken through the soil, to blossom in the May sunshine. From where has it drawn its food and water for this miraculous becoming? Can you name any particular aspects of the soil of your circumstances that you can see now, with hindsight, have provided that food and water, even though it may not have felt like that at the time?

7. YOUR HISTORY, YOUR MYSTERY

Praying our stories

Using the stilling and relaxing skills we looked at in Chapter 3, let's just spend a few moments listening to a *story*. Just try reading these two short paragraphs, and see which one of them 'speaks' to you. Don't bother about their content. Just notice your 'gut reaction' to what you are reading. For example, is it boring or interesting, meaningful to you or just something you will forget as soon as you have read it?

> *During the years 1945 to 1989 East Germany was a separate state under Soviet occupation. It was ruled by a communist puppet government. By 1961 so many people were fleeing to the West that the authorities closed the borders and built the infamous Berlin Wall to prevent people going from East to West. Young people hoping to enter higher education were required to join the Communist party. It was a grave crime to try to leave East Germany for a western country and many thousands of refugees were killed in the attempt. In November 1989, in an uprising of all the Communist totalitarian countries of Eastern Europe, the Soviet stranglehold was broken. In Berlin the uprising led to the breaching of the Berlin Wall on 9 November and the re-unification of East and West Germany followed in 1990.*

Now listen to a rather different way of looking at these facts of history:

> *Peter was born in the middle of the war, in the Eastern part of Berlin. When only a baby he experienced the howling of the bombers overhead and remembers how his parents would carry him to the air raid shelters. When he was nineteen he realised that he wasn't going to be allowed to stay at University unless he joined the Communist party. Events speeded up dramatically at that time, and he found himself confronted by a snap decision. On 12 August 1961 it was rumoured that something was about to happen along the borders. He took his chance and, with nothing more than his*

swimming trunks, he swam across the Teltow Canal, that ran along the east-west border through Berlin, and asked for political asylum in the West. The next day the borders were closed behind him and it was to be nineteen years before he saw his mother again. His cousin, Konrad, stayed behind in the East. But he too was destined to cross the border in a dramatic way. On 9 November 1989 East Berlin was buzzing with rumour: something was happening along the borders. Konrad went off to see what was going on. When he arrived at the Wall he couldn't believe his eyes. Half of Berlin seemed to have gathered there. People were going across to the West! The border was open! The guards stood there bemused, not knowing what to do about it. He drove from East to West Berlin in his old Trabi, and someone poured a bottle of champagne over the car as he drove through the open checkpoint. The two cousins met up again soon afterwards – an emotional reunion. They hugged each other in silence, both too choked to speak. Their story was history!

Now just stop to consider for a moment: which of these two accounts of post-war life in Germany do you relate to more? Which one is more likely to stick in your memory?

Jesus habitually used stories to teach us about the Kingdom. If you read the Gospels you will find whole books full of stories. And what kind of 'theology' do we relate to more easily do you think? The theology that spells out the moral principles and the theories of redemption that underlie our faith, or the story that begins: 'There was once a carpenter's son in Nazareth ....'? I would suggest that the beginning – and the whole purpose – of our journey with God lies in our *story*. The meaning and destination of our lives lies in the way in which *our story* connects to Jesus and the *Gospel story* of redemption.

So I would like to invite you to reflect on your story, because that is, I believe, where you will most easily find the traces of God's action in your life.

Discovering your story

When our daughter was in primary school she was given an exercise in plotting the family history as far as she could. We knew that we had information about her ancestors going back, in two strands of the family (one German and one Scottish), for about 200 years, so we helped her to explore this project by drawing a 'time line'. On one side of the line we marked the main events in world history (such as the invention of electricity and the motor car) and in European history especially (such as the two world wars, the building of the Berlin Wall, etc.). On the other side of the time line we marked significant events in the family, including the birth and death of all the family members we could trace. Now, as I look back, I realise that we were actually connecting our family story with the world story, in doing this. And now I also realise how helpful it can be to do something similar to connect the outward and obvious facts of our lives with the underlying movements in our hearts that reveal to us where God is for us and how he is forming us.

You might like to try this as an exercise in prayer. You could begin by making a note of the important events in your own life: your birth, starting school, changes of school, student times, jobs, important relationships, marriage, the birth of children, of grandchildren, the names of friends, places where you have lived, holidays that you especially remember, and so on. You could call this the *visible* side of your time line.

So far so good. Now turn to the *invisible* side of your story – those things that no outside observer would notice, but which may turn out to be the most significant things of all. For this part of the exercise, begin by asking God to open the eyes of your heart to see where the most life-giving and life-changing points in your story have been. This is truly an exercise in prayer. Don't try to force your own memory, but turn instead to God's grace, and trust him to bring you to an awareness of what he is inviting you to remember. Some examples of these 'inner landmarks' might be: events or encounters that caused some 'change of heart' inside you and made you see things from a different perspective; moments when perhaps the world 'stood still' for you, and you felt 'touched by God'; times of particular darkness when you felt abandoned by God; people who have been 'wisdom figures' for you, or who have profoundly influenced your inner journey.

Now try noticing particular moments that were life-giving. How do you feel these moments have made a difference to your life since they happened? And those events that seemed destructive at the time – have they actually destroyed you? With hindsight, can you see any way in which these dark patches of your experience have led you to new 'growth spurts'? What do you most relish in your experience? And what do you most regret? Let them both be there, simply laid bare before God in your prayer. Don't try to suppress the feelings you may have about them. Let your joy be joy and let your tears be shed. This kind of prayer is truly an intimate encounter with the Lord and it will become a source of renewed energy for you.

When your personal story becomes connected like this, in your heart, with the story of redemption, you are coming close to the heart of the meaning of your life, and discovering that that meaning is part of the meaning of the whole of God's creation and his redeeming life. Like the two cousins in Berlin, your story becomes *his*-story, and his story – of creation and redemption – holds *your* story in the palm of his hands.

A patchwork quilt

Another memory from our daughter's primary school days is the gift the school gave to the headmistress when she retired. A few months before the retirement date, the teachers asked everyone in their classes to make a little 'patch', and embroider their own name on it. The patches were then collected and sewn together to make a quilt for the headmistress, whom they all loved and respected. The children threw themselves into the task with enthusiasm, and the resulting quilt was a delight to them all. Like Joseph's dreamcoat, it was made of a little bit of every child, and it literally brought the headmistress to tears when she saw it. Every patch, when she looked at it, brought to life again a child she had cherished in her own particular way. And the whole quilt, made up of her memories, would keep her warm in the years ahead.

A good way to get in touch with your story is to collect your own 'patches' like this. A 'patch' can be whatever comes to your mind as you reflect back over the flow of your life: special moments and significant relationships; journeys you have made; turning points; changes in your lifestyle; places that you return to in memory; regrets and sorrows; joys and enthusiasms. Anything and everything might turn up among your patches. But the point of the patches is to bring them together into a *wholeness* that is *you*. Your 'story' is like the quilt that comes to be when your patches come together. It is absolutely unique, and crammed full of meaning and of a beauty all its own. And if that headmistress dissolved into tears of joy when she saw her pupils' gift, how do you think God is going to respond when you bring him the precious patchwork of *your* life?

The quilt is about wholeness, and the coming together of all that is *you*, to make something that is greater than the sum of its parts. And that new thing that your life is weaving is not just for yourself. It is becoming a quilt for the warming and holding of others. Your story is God's story, lived out in you, and it is also *our* story, the story of the whole human family, which cannot be complete until *your* part of it is told and welcomed.

TAKING IT FURTHER . . .

During the next few days or weeks, try to take a little time in prayer just to remember your life and your journey of faith so far. There are all kinds of ways to do this. A few are suggested here, but you may prefer to find your own individual way of recalling the people, events, conversations, meetings and other experiences that stand out in your memory as *life-changing* times . . ..

- You might like to imagine your life as a river. It would be more true to describe your actual *life* as the river-banks, and the journey of your innermost self as the flow of the river between those banks until it reaches its destination in the sea. Sometimes this flow may have seemed calm and restful, sometimes it may have had to negotiate rocks, dams and other obstructions. You may feel that your 'innermost self' has sometimes gone underground, and out of sight, even to yourself, and there may have been times when it felt dried up and lost in the wilderness. You may find it helpful to reflect on those people, places and experiences that were 'tributaries' to your inner river, and express your gratitude to God for these gifts. And of course you will have your own feelings about the nature of the 'sea' which is the ultimate destination of your 'river'. Just let all these possibilities be present in your thoughts and your prayers for a while, and maybe jot down any thoughts or memories that seem especially important to you.
- Another picture of the 'inner journey' is to imagine a pathway climbing up a mountain. What difficulties does the path run into, and what special 'views' along the way have left you with a sense of joy and wonder? What signposts have been helpful to you? What major milestones do

Where did your path come from and where is it leading?

you feel you have passed, and how do you feel about them? What important discoveries have there been along the path? Where did the path begin and where is it leading you? What 'baggage' are you carrying, and do you ever wish it were not so heavy? Which companions have been alongside you at different times, as you have been walking your path? What landmarks have guided you on your journey?

- We believe, as Christians, that Jesus walks alongside us on our life's path, but does this truth really mean anything to us *in practice*? If we look at the Gospel we can find a journey made by two people very much like ourselves. They were walking to the village of Emmaus, not far from Jerusalem, after the events of Good Friday, and were feeling about as low as it is possible to get. They had pinned all their hopes on Jesus, the Messiah, and now he had been put to death as a common criminal. The sense of disillusionment and despair must have been overwhelming for them. Then a stranger comes up alongside them and they fall into conversation with him. He appears to be the only person around who hasn't heard about the events of the Passover in Jerusalem. But he notices their despair and he gently draws them to trust him and share *their* story with him. Imagine that you are one of those travellers. Let the gentle stranger come up beside you and draw you into conversation. He asks about *your* story, and why you are making this journey. He asks how you *feel* about the events of your own life's story, and how you are feeling now. *Tell him* in your prayer. Don't be afraid to show him your negative feelings as well as the happier memories. After a while you come to a cross-roads. The stranger appears to be going straight on, but night is falling and you need to stop over in the inn. How do you feel about your walk with the stranger? What happens next in your imagination? You will find this story in Luke 24:13–35.

8. ACTION REPLAY

Reviewing the day with God

The golden thread

For a period of about nine months recently I was visiting a sick friend and his wife each week, to take them Holy Communion. The man was dying of cancer and was literally fading away before our eyes, and his wife was looking after him, and making this last journey in faith alongside him, knowing that very soon they would be parted. In the end he died just a few weeks before their golden wedding anniversary.

Although it was harrowing in many ways to see these friends every week in the process of facing death and all its fears and the anguish of impending loss, I used to look forward very much to these weekly visits. When I arrived, we would sit down together, the three of us, after we had held the Eucharistic service, and my friend would invariably say: 'Let's tell Margaret about the things that have been really good during this week.' And I would sit and listen as they shared with me a story, perhaps, of someone who had visited and brought them a piece of news, or a new insight or perspective on the world, or maybe one of them had been reading something that moved them and that they wanted to share.

Almost no week passed without my coming away with a book they had lent me, or a poem or an article that they had photocopied, for me to read. Perhaps they would have received a letter, or maybe a new flower had come out in the garden, or they had spotted a visiting bird. Often the remembered good thing was a flash of memory that one of them had experienced, or a dream that had left them feeling calm and at peace, or simply an act of kindness – a neighbour had called, a son or daughter had phoned, the nurse had been gentle, the postman had shared a joke …. Then they would turn to me, and ask about my week, and invite me to share my remembered treasure.

In these months I began to see, from them, that it was possible, whatever the outward circumstances of life, to discover a *golden thread* running through each day. There might only be one thing that shone out with that sparkle, but there *would* be one thing, if we opened our eyes to see, and that one thing was infinitely worth searching for. It was a gift from God. And I know now, with hindsight, that this approach to the presence of God in their daily lives was changing those months from what might have been a time of agony and despair and self-pity, into a time of amazing, outflowing awareness and joy.

In the last chapter we looked back together over the flow of our own personal life's story, and where God has been in it. Now I would like to invite you to bring the focus in a bit closer and try reviewing the day, or perhaps the week, in the same kind of way, with an eye constantly open to spot the golden thread. The practice of reviewing the day, prayerfully, with God, in this way, has come down to us through countless generations of Christians. There is nothing new or revolutionary about it. In this prayer you are in the company of millions of Christians, all down the centuries. But it *could* cause a revolution in your way of looking at *your* 'ordinary', everyday life.

Colour your day

Having recognised a golden thread in your day (or in your week, if that is easier for you at first), you might like to try filling in some of the other 'colours' that have been around for you. Your passing moods may help you with this. As you look back over the day, and re-play the events and encounters that you have had, try to notice how you were feeling, as the day went on.

- What were the main moods of your day?
- What elated you, what left you feeling let down? What made you angry?
- Did anything give rise to a surge of joy inside you?

Can you begin to see where the real roots of these feelings may lie? For example, a feeling of unease or distress around a particular event in your day may be revealing some 'unfinished business', or some damaged relationship that, subconsciously, you sense you need to attend to. If so, lay it before God, honestly, and without disguises, in your prayer and simply ask for his healing and listen, with your heart, to whatever suggestions arise inside you. They may be showing you a new way forward in dealing with the problem.

Or your moods of elation may be pointing to aspects of your life that are helping you to grow and are nourishing a sense of joy and genuine well-being in you. Notice these moods, and, again, try to follow them through to their deeper roots. Let them lead you deep down to the sources of what is truly life-giving in your day-by-day experience. Thank God for these things in your life and ask him to help you draw on them more and more deeply, so that they may become increasingly life-giving for yourself and for those around you – your family, friends, colleagues and neighbours.

Are there any dark patches?

When I used to visit my dying friend, I knew perfectly well that he would have experienced times of darkness in his week. It would have been dishonest to pretend that the whole week had ever been one long 'golden thread'. Now, as I look back to those visits, I realise that the 'darkness' used to be expressed during the Eucharistic service itself, as we shared a time of prayer together and asked God for his healing touch on whatever had been 'out of order', in ourselves or in the world around us, during the week. At those times, nobody needed to say very much aloud about the darkness they had experienced in their hearts. We would just express very simply any feeling of pain, fear, guilt or inadequacy that we recalled from the week. Nobody would make any comment. The 'dark patch' would simply be received and acknowledged in a loving silence between us, and laid before God.

As you look back over the day, you may notice incidents where you feel that you failed to respond to God's love, or to another person's needs, in some particular way. Tell him how you feel. Ask him to shine the light of his love in those particular places, even though that light may hurt your eyes and make you cry. Trust that he will enlighten your darkness with gentleness and love. Express sorrow for anything that still grieves you, and ask for the grace to begin again tomorrow with a lightened heart and renewed courage.

If you make this 'action replay' prayer at the end of the day, end it by committing yourself, and all those you love, into his care, as a child might fall asleep in its mother's arms.

If all else fails . . .

Let me just leave you with two suggestions for staying close to God in prayer even – and especially – at times when you feel 'unable to pray', or when it has been 'one of those days' and all you want to do is forget about it and fall asleep.

We all experience times when prayer feels, frankly, miles away and quite out of reach. If you find yourself in a phase like this, and there is no time, or no inclination for any other kind of prayer, try at least to spend just a few minutes before you fall asleep, re-playing the main events and feelings of your day, as you might re-run a video in 'fast forward' until something catches your attention and you slow the action down, to attend to it more carefully. Just notice those moments that 'grab' you and let them be present, in your memory, and before God.

This kind of prayer, which many call the '*Review of the Day*' (you may also meet it under the name of the '*Examen*' or '*The Review of Consciousness*'), has the power to touch the whole of your day with your unspoken desire to discover God's presence in it. You will find that it soon becomes a habit that will increase your awareness of God's presence in your whole life.

And if you don't have the time, or the energy, to re-play your whole day like this, try noticing 'just one thing' that you would like to say 'Thank you' to God for. I can remember going to work one morning. The office was in a very desolate and run-down place in Manchester. I was feeling depressed in myself, and dreading the day ahead. As I walked from the station, through the grim backstreets, and past derelict and half-demolished buildings, my physical surroundings seemed to be echoing back my own mood to me. Then all at once, as I walked along, head down, hoping not to be mugged as I went, I noticed a glorious clump of clover blooming triumphantly among the rubble, and a huge bumble bee, gathering nectar from it in this, the most unpromising place it was possible to imagine. *That* was my 'just one thing' to thank God for that day, and I have never forgotten that somehow, somewhere, there is always a clump of clover among the rubble of our lives, if we open our eyes to see as God sees.

Somehow, somewhere,
there is always a clump of clover.

TAKING IT FURTHER . . .

To help you feel comfortable with this kind of prayer, you might like to try this imaginative exercise:

Find a comfortable place to sit, and maybe close your eyes, or focus your gaze, perhaps on a candle. Relax and let the tensions of the day slip away for a few minutes.

The children are in bed and the last protests or requests for drinks, or for comfort in the nightmares have subsided. The TV offerings are un-inspiring. The day has been . . .. How *has* the day been?

Try to imagine this scene in your own home. Into the midst of the evening reveries, when the panics of the day have been resolved, or perhaps when the aching loneliness of a day without human contact or human hope has been lived through, the phone rings.

Imagine picking up the phone – perhaps with excitement, perhaps with irritation – and hear a warm, concerned and gentle voice say: 'I just called to ask how your day has been . . .. Tell me about it. Tell me how you are. Tell me how you feel . . ..'

In your imagination, take the phone to your favourite chair. Switch off the TV or find a place for yourself somewhere else in a quiet corner. Settle yourself for this, most welcome of phone calls. Curl up and relax. And the call is free. You can talk for as long as you like.

Begin by simply savouring the fact that your friend has called you. 'I have called you *friend*,' he reassures you. 'And I'm so glad that you have taken the time to pick up the receiver and give us these minutes together, just the two of us.' It occurs to you that, though he is your closest friend, you have scarcely given him a thought all day. But *he* has not forgotten *you*, and he is here to tell you just that.

How does the conversation go on? Perhaps you might first bring to mind the *blessings* of the day. What has happened to make you want to thank him? Has there been a meeting with someone, or a letter or a friendly, unexpected word or gesture? Has anything made you laugh? Have you solved some problem that may have been niggling you? Have you had any opportunity just to notice something good in the world around you, maybe some special aspect of the natural world, a lovely sunset, a refreshing shower for the garden, a momentary break in the cloud cover, revealing a patch of blue sky?

You might like to remember, in your prayer, all those who have deserved your gratitude today. Those who grew the food you have eaten, those who picked the tea that you have drunk. Those who have faithfully supplied the essential services. Those who have done something for you that they didn't need to do. And finally – and you may not find this easy – remember something about yourself and your day that you can be proud about! Then hear your friend's voice saying 'Well done!'

The things that have come to mind in this way are the facts and feelings of your day, and the raw materials of your prayer. Pause for a moment and just ask your friend to help you to see how his love for you has been working in these facts and these feelings.

Now spend a few minutes reflecting peacefully on what you have recalled, trusting that the light of awareness of God's action in your day has been given. Let him speak to your heart in whatever way he will. Notice, for example:

- What has drawn you closer to God today?
- What have you learned about him and about the way his Kingdom works?
- What happened to make you feel loved today, and were you able to give a sign of love to another person?
- What kind of moods were present in your day? Just notice them, without any judgement. Pour out your reactions to your friend on the phone. It's OK to tell him about how angry you were with the neighbour, how impatient with the children, how frustrated at missing a chance to give your boss a piece of your mind, how unaccountably moved you felt when that postcard came from an old friend, how relieved at some unexpected offer of help, how helpless in the face of some suffering you have witnessed. It's OK to tell him that the day has been unspeakably awful and that all you can say for it is that you are glad it's over.
- Is there any 'unfinished business' that you would like to raise – maybe something that has left you feeling inadequate or displeased with yourself or with someone else, or fearful for the consequences still to come?

These are just a few examples of things you might want to mention to your friend. Simply express whatever is in your heart, in whatever way feels right for you. Say as much or as little as you like, because in the end this conversation isn't about words. It is a heart-to-heart encounter.

Before you put the receiver down, spend a few moments looking forward to tomorrow, and ask your friend to open your eyes and ears to see and notice everything he wants to reveal to you of himself in its hours and its events. Ask him to make you alert to his surprises, and to his presence in everyone you will meet.

And be sure, before you end the conversation, to hear his words of blessing: 'Goodnight my child, I love you. I bless you. Sleep in peace.'

For a very good introduction to this form of prayer, see *Sleeping with Bread* by Dennis, Sheila and Matthew Linn (Paulist Press, 1995).

9. WITH LOVE AND PRAYERS . . .

The prayer of intercession

Do you ever end a letter with these or similar words? I often do it myself, and when I do I mean what I say. I really mean that I will be holding that person in my prayer. But what, if anything, do I mean by that? What good do 'my prayers' do for the person I am writing to? Does my promise to pray for them offer anything more than a warm feeling that someone is thinking of them – no bad thing in itself, of course, but is it *prayer*?

I have struggled greatly with this problem through the years, and seriously wondered what intercessory prayer can mean, in the presence of a God who knows the needs of those we pray for far better than we ever could. We can reel off a list of names and requests like a checklist that may leave us feeling satisfied that we have 'prayed for' the people on the list, but have we actually done anything at all? And what, if anything, could we do more than that?

Journeying to the centre

One way that helps me make some sense of intercessory prayer is a mental picture I have of the human family as the circumference of a vast circle. Each of us has a place on this circumference, just as we have a place on the surface of the earth. We feel close to some people who seem to be 'in the same place' as we are on the circle of life, and we feel literally diametrically opposed to others, who happen to be (in terms of their opinions, or temperament or even their spirituality) on the opposite side of the circle.

But the whole circle is centred on God, in whom it has its entire existence. God is the hub around which it all spins. When we go into prayer, we are at the very least signalling our *desire* to be with him in that centre. We discover that the deepest centre of ourselves is in some mysterious way, beyond our understanding, also the centre who is God. Our own truest self is a particle of God's self. To pray is to bring ourselves into resonance with that universal centre. The music that flows from that resonance will affect not just ourselves but everything and everyone around us.

If this picture works for you, it might now be possible to see that when you pray for particular individuals and their needs you are doing two things:

- You are, as it were, gathering them from around the circumference of this circle (perhaps from nearby, perhaps from far away), first of all into your own thoughts. When you mention each name, you are consciously and deliberately bringing that person into your mind.
- You are then bringing yourself and those you have gathered down to the centre of yourself, to the still and silent place where you know yourself to be one with God.

What happens there, in the deep centre of things, need not concern us. A familiar scene may bring it closer: imagine, perhaps, that the year has dragged on with little let-up in a trail of bad weather. It gets to August. Children are fractious and bad-tempered. Elderly relatives are pale and depressed. You yourself would give anything for a break and a glimpse of the sun. Then the weather suddenly takes a turn for the better. The skies clear. The temperature rises. The sun smiles. You gather your flock into the car, buckets and spades included. You collect Granddad en route and off you go to the coast.

You could have gone on your own. But it mattered to you that they too had a season in the sun. As you relax on the beach, knowing that the children are revelling in this space of sun and sand and sea, and that Granddad will relish the memory of this day through many wintry months ahead, you don't need to analyse *why* this day is good for all of them. Enough to know that it *is*.

I think something similar happens when we pray for others. We take them with us, as it were, into the radiance of God's presence, and we don't need to know why that is a good thing to do, or how it may be affecting their deepest being. We just know that it *is*.

Bedrock connections

I am always fascinated by the fact that, though we see our world as a series of islands and continents, set in vast tracts of ocean, and our maps reflect this understanding, yet if we can imagine the tide going out, radically and universally, we would see the obvious fact that all our islands and continents are just a single lump of rock, beneath the tideline.

In the Book of Revelation, St John tells us that in the new heaven and the new earth 'there is no more sea'. This may be bad news to those who, like me, love the sea in all its shapes and forms, but in the Jewish world–view the sea was seen as the container of all that was evil, or threatening. And certainly, whatever our feelings about the sea, it is a fact that it is what separates our islands and continents and obscures the reality of our bedrock oneness.

'No man is an island' it is said. Yet it is also true that we all live our lives for the most part *as if we were islands*. We tend to guard and cherish our separateness from everyone else, and live from a centre of gravity within ourselves, rather than from the deep, and true, centre of gravity in the heart of our wholeness and oneness. But in prayer, we might say, 'the tide goes out'. We shift our inner centre of gravity from ourselves to God. We get a glimpse of the bedrock union in which we all have our eternal being.

What might this mean for intercessory prayer? For me, I think, it means that I am brought face to face with the fact that I and the woman next door, the colleague at the next desk, the drug-pusher in the magistrates' court and his victim in the rehab. centre are all made of the same stuff. We are one in the bedrock. Although this realisation doesn't, of course, change anything in the way God sees us and cares for us, it certainly changes *our* perspectives. Now it becomes clear that *their* joys and their pain, their saintliness or sinfulness is intimately, inseparably one with our own. When we pray for someone, if we do so genuinely and with a real desire to be with them in this bedrock reality, we meet them face to face, not on our terms, or on theirs, but on God's. The real test of such prayer is this: will we remember the bedrock oneness that we share, when the tide comes in and we are islands again, tempted to rebuild the fences between us?

'At home' with God

One thing that especially helps me to pray for others is to make an effort to become familiar with their physical surroundings. Once I know a person's home environment, or if I have been with them in a place that they love, it becomes much easier to go there in my prayer, taking the Lord with me (or, rather, letting *him* take *me*). It makes deep sense of Jesus' promise that 'where two or more are gathered in my name I am there in the midst of them'.

In my 'prayer space' and my 'prayer time' I can be with the one I pray for in a very real, intimate, familiar way, and know that the two of us are in the Lord's presence.

Taking the trouble to get to know a person on their home ground brings other benefits too:

• It forces me to focus more on *the other person's* real needs, and not on my desire to 'be helpful' on my own terms. It shifts the centre of gravity to their place and away from my own.
• It shows up in a real, solid way, the place, and maybe even the means through which my prayers may be answered in practical ways. If I know the person's living space I am much more likely to notice where her practical needs are centred.

Being 'at home' with God starts with a call to be 'at home' with each other.

Bringing back God's answers

There is a village in Derbyshire which, in 1665 and 1666 was almost wiped out by the Bubonic Plague. It is famous because at that time the villagers made a deliberate, collective and courageous decision to isolate themselves, in order to protect the surrounding neighbourhood from contagion. During this terrible time, they would collect their supplies of food, medication and news of the outside world, from the boundary stones that marked the circumference of the isolation zone.

Whenever I walk along the path between the village and one of these boundary stones, I am very moved by the memory of these people. I imagine perhaps the one remaining healthy member of a stricken family trudging along this path to collect the food and medication and letters left at the boundary stone by their benefactors from the surrounding villages. I am even more moved when I turn back from the stone and retrace my steps back to the village. That one healthy person, still capable of making the life-giving journey to the boundary stone, could so easily have stayed there, or slipped off into the surrounding hills to safety. But he turned back instead, back to the village, putrid with the smell of death, bringing back

*Someone who knows the way,
who will make the journey on their behalf,
and come back to them in their need.*

the means of life from the boundary. Back into the risk of contagion. Back to the mute suffering of the plague victims. Back to the ones who did not have the strength to help themselves.

This, for me, is what it means to pray for each other. It means to co-operate with God in answering these prayers. It means turning our pleas into action. The plague villagers trusted that the means of life would indeed be brought to the boundary stones. But they also needed someone who knew the way, and had the strength to make the journey on their behalf. And they needed someone who would come back to them in their need, however tempting it might be to stay forever 'with the Lord' and overlook our own responsibilities in his desire for our salvation.

Becoming the answer to your prayers

St John, in his Gospel, describes a scene at the Pool of Bethesda in Jerusalem (in John 5:1–13). This poolside was frequented by people in dire need of healing. John mentions in particular 'the blind, the lame and the paralysed'. They would congregate there because there was a tradition that when the waters were stirred (by an angel it was believed), the first person to reach the pool would be healed.

Some years ago now I had been spending quite some time listening to the story of someone who had been searching for a real and personal relationship with God all his life. Eventually he asked me to be with him in a local church, during his first attempt to meet God in imaginative prayer (see also Chapter 16), and I suggested this passage to him as a focus for his prayer, little realising the implications it would have for both of us.

Rather reluctantly I went to the church with him, feeling that actually it would have been better for him to be alone. Once there I found a quiet corner in the church, some distance away from him, and sat down to wait alongside him. It took me a few minutes even to come to the thought that it might be a good thing to pray for him and with him at this significant time. At first my prayers for him were the only kind of intercessory prayer I knew. I simply lobbed my requests over the fence at God, asking him to do what needed to be done for this man, and to give him the healing he was asking for.

Almost in spite of myself, however, I found that I too was being drawn into imaginative prayer, and where else would I go, in the circumstances, but to the Pool of Bethesda. Again, I sat down at the poolside to wait for my friend. A patient observer? Or an observer of the patient? Until, in my prayer, Jesus approached me, sat down beside me and drew me into conversation.

'What do you think they are doing here?' he asked me.

That was easy. 'They are waiting to be healed,' I replied. 'When the angel stirs the water, one of them will go in and be healed.'

'What is wrong with them?' Jesus continued.

'Some are blind and others are paralysed', I told him.

'So how will any of them get to the pool when the water is stirred?' he asked me. 'Surely those who are blind won't see that the water has been stirred, and the ones who are paralysed will see it but they won't be able to move.'

The simple logic confounded me, and I had an uneasy feeling that Jesus had meant it to! He smiled, with a gentle determination:

'No-one will reach the healing water alone. They all need someone who will take them. They need someone else's eyes and limbs.'

This was the first time – the first of many – when Jesus challenged me to become the answer to my own prayers of intercession. Teresa of Avila reminds us that he has no hands on earth now but ours, no eyes, no limbs but ours. If we ask him to act on behalf of others we must be willing to become the implements of that action. Perhaps our reluctance to do so is the reason why so many of our intercessions seem to remain unanswered.

TAKING IT FURTHER ...

Cast your mind back over the past week or so. Can you name any of the people you have been praying for? You might even like to jot their names down on a piece of paper and remind yourself of why you have been praying for them (but do destroy the paper afterwards, to protect their confidentiality).

Just take a few minutes to look very closely at what you have been asking God to do for them. Maybe focus on just one or two people who are often in your prayers. What are you actually hoping he will do for those people? Is there any way that you can at least make a start on the job yourself? Asking God to heal a person who suffers from chronic, debilitating depression may be asking him for a miracle that begins with a single friendly smile, or a loving letter or phone call, or a generous gift of an hour out of a busy day to visit someone whose hours are like eternities. We so often hold back from making the first step because we cannot imagine where the road will lead from there.

As a way of connecting to that deep centre of reality where we are truly 'all one', you might like to try an exercise that often helps me. Think of a group of people in which you feel at home. They may be people you share your faith with, or a group you enjoy some hobby or sport with or just a circle of friends. No doubt through the years new people have joined the group and others have gone away. Tomorrow, for all you know, a new person may come along, someone you have never seen before, but before long that person may have become a valued friend.

And now the exercise: next time you are out in town, at the shops, on the road behind the steering wheel, or anywhere surrounded by strangers, notice your feelings. All too often, I find personally, I feel impatient with the crowds around me, and irritated when they slow me down or hold me up or get in my way. When this happens I sometimes (I wish I could say 'always') try looking into one or two of the faces of these strangers, and seeing, instead of a nuisance in my way, the face of the person who might be the next to join my 'group'.

For example, I am sometimes involved in helping to give retreats in daily life, often in parishes where I know no-one. When the outside world is getting on top of me on a busy Saturday morning, I sometimes stop to reflect that the next face I see might be arriving at the next parish retreat. Immediately, I find, I see that person differently. I assume the best about him, instead of the worst. I assume that he is searching for God, and for meaning, and is a person of good will, where only minutes earlier I had been looking upon him as someone whose whole aim in life was to get in front of me at the fish counter. In short, I see him, however briefly, *as he really is*, and not as an extension of my own impatience. Just a small way of meeting each other in the 'bedrock wholeness', perhaps, but a method that can be easily practised, wherever we find ourselves.

10. TWO COLUMN INCHES

Bringing the world's events to God

A particular form of intercessory prayer, and one which can frequently flow most powerfully out of our own experience of pain, is to 'pray the news'.

This means taking complete strangers, or whole groups of people or other situations from the national or international news into your prayer – into that centre where we are all one.

Is it in any way meaningful to pray for situations that are completely beyond our control and have no direct bearing on our own life's journey ...? Or have they? If it is true that we are 'all one below the tideline', whatever happens in Northern Ireland, or Iran, or Croatia is as much part of our being-in-the-world as *our* affairs are part of what makes other people who they are. A blight on one branch of the tree has an effect on the tree as a whole and, therefore, on every other branch. A virus that affects our lungs will sooner or later lower the resistance and strength of every other part of the body.

And if it is meaningful to pray in such a way, how might we approach this kind of prayer? In this chapter we will look at two ways of 'praying the news' that you might like to try, and then go on to reflect on the very special power such prayer has when it flows from the heart of someone who has a real bond of empathy with the situation being prayed for. Finally, we will look at ways of living out the dream towards which our prayer might beckon us, on behalf of those we pray for.

The expanding universe method
This approach to praying the news begins in your own backyard. Try reading your local newspaper, or your parish magazine, or perhaps even something less 'official', like the noticeboard in the village post office or the posters in your High Street.

Let's take the local paper as a starting point. Just try noticing the issues that seem to be dominating peoples' thoughts and attention right now in your own local area. What, as the doctor might ask you, seems to be the trouble? Are there any natural or environmental problems in the news? Have your local politicians been making waves with recent decisions? Is there a particular crime that has roused a lot of emotion? Are any controversies brewing? What are they about?

In my own town at present, for example, there are plans to build a by-pass road which will make the journey to work much easier and faster for a few people, but will go straight past a school playground, putting children at risk both of cars and of their fumes. A common dilemma, but in this particular case there is an extra parameter that makes the whole issue into quite a cliff-hanger: a local church owns a crucial few yards of land, without which the by-pass cannot be built, and for which no compulsory purchase order is permitted. The parishioners, and indeed many other local people, have made it clear to the parish priest that they do not approve the sale of this bit of land, and the priest, having canvassed this local opinion, has now put the people's case to the diocese. It remains to be seen how the diocese will decide . . . .

Why should such a relatively minor matter cause you to hammer on heaven's door with your own prayers of intercession on behalf of either the by-pass or the playground? One good reason suggests itself. This minor, local issue calls for discernment and decision-making which are a small, *but accessible*, fragment of much larger, more far-reaching decisions that potentially affect the well-being of all creation. It demands that we face, here on our own doorstep, questions about what we really want, what we most value, and how we exercise what little power we have. We know that we can't, single-handed, save the rainforests or prevent the oppression of minority peoples by those who hold power over them. But the people of that parish know that they *can* tell their parish priest what they think, and they can also make sure that their feelings get heard by those who will make the decision. A drop in the ocean, perhaps. But what else is the ocean, if not a vast collection of drops?

Local action of this kind has a number of positive effects:

- It can achieve a change of heart in the real decision-makers.
- It can make good things happen, or prevent bad things from happening.

Conversely, of course, if this local power is not wielded with wisdom and with love, it can do just the opposite, making bad things happen and preventing the good.

- It can empower ordinary people to exercise their own judgement, and accept a degree of responsibility, in matters that affect us all.
- It can harness the ideals and dreams of these same 'ordinary' people on behalf of those who have no vote about how things are done: the children, the frail, the marginalised, the inarticulate.

In short, it can become a sign, and an effective sign, of the coming of the reign of God. It matters, how we respond at this local level. It matters because it makes a real difference to what happens locally. But it also matters because local decisions have global consequences that we can almost never see or imagine at the time. Just as children, learning their multiplication tables at school cannot imagine the many real-life situations ahead of them when they will need such knowledge, so, when we involve ourselves in local issues, we cannot begin to imagine their effects on the whole human family. We throw our pebble of involvement into the village pond and it contributes to a tidal wave of reaction on beaches at the other end of the world. It *matters*, how we throw our pebble! Will it be the pebble that clogs up the wheels of life, or the pebble that slays the oppressor-Goliath?

And so, a way to pray the news might be to reflect, over time, on a particular local issue that rouses your feelings in some way, and to let it grow until you begin to see something of its global consequences. Notice, for example, what factors are influencing your own feelings, and how these same factors re-appear again and again, in different guises, in the big stories of international significance. Notice your own reactions, and then ask yourself: 'Is my response likely to lead me, and others, to an *increase* of faith, hope and love, or is it more likely to lead to a *decrease*? You can be sure that whatever increases the reign of love in your own home town will also increase it in the wider world, though you may never know through what invisible channels that power will flow.

And finally, when you find reactions in yourself that *do* seem to be leading closer to the reign of God, *act on them* . . . for all our sakes!

The shrinking world method

It is very easy to become quite overwhelmed by the international news, and to be sucked down into an abyss of despair when we become aware of our own apparent helplessness to change things, or even to alleviate the world's suffering in any significant way. A common, and understandable reaction in these circumstances is to switch off inwardly – to insulate ourselves against an encroachment of grief and pain that we cannot bear. It follows, all too easily, that we become quite inured to some of the horrors we see on our television screens. We can grow dangerously apathetic and detached. If your reactions are anything like mine, when this happens, you start to feel bad about yourself for not feeling particularly bad about what is happening to others in the world. Guilt kicks in, and undermines any hope of the possibility of releasing any positive energy into the troubled situation.

When I find myself reacting like this, I notice that it helps to take advantage of what the news editors call the 'human interest factor'. In practice this means paying real attention to the very specific situation of a particular person or family caught up in the trouble. There is ample scope for trying out this way of 'being with' people in prayer. Every night there is a report from somewhere around the world of a natural disaster, or a political crisis or a major atrocity or ferocious crime. Instead of becoming submerged in your reactions of horror, or fear, or disgust, try instead to notice the face of someone caught in the middle of it. Notice the expression in their eyes. Feel, in your imagination, the cold sweat of their fear. See for yourself where they are living. Notice the things they say. Enter into their personal domestic space for a while and let it become your prayer, just as you might pray for a friend.

I remember when the hostility between Serbs and Croats in the former Yugoslavia was at its height, feeling shamefully unmoved by much that I was seeing and hearing in the daily news. Until one day I caught a snatch of conversation recorded by a reporter . . . .

I was listening to the car radio. The horrifying statistics from Bosnia were passing through my brain, but not really touching my heart. It was too much to cope with, and I knew I was screening it out. Then a woman's voice came over the air. She was saying how much easier it would have been if they were fighting an enemy, and not those who had seemed to be friends. She was fighting people she had been drinking coffee with only a few weeks ago, she said.

It went straight to somewhere deep in my gut. My feelings locked into hers for a few split seconds, and I knew that I could pray for her in a real way. I could be with her over the coffee and in the shell-fire, sharing something of her bitterness and despair. I could bring her pain to God, because she was too pre-occupied to bring it herself. I understand about drinking coffee and I understand about friends who turn sour on you. It wasn't much of a connection, but it was enough to connect us in prayer, and it was *real*.

So another way of praying the news, especially when the news is all too much for you, might be to seek out a real person amid the carnage, and let that one person's story, that one person's need, form your prayer of intercession. This will shrink the unmanageable down to a size that is unavoidable. It will hurt, but real prayer like this maybe *has* to hurt, just as Christ's prayer for us from the cross was a hurting prayer.

When redundancy shook our personal securities for the first time a few years ago, I remember being deeply moved by a small, hand-made card from a friend. It read:

> *I am only one,*
> *but I am one.*
> *I cannot do everything,*
> *but I can do something.*
> *What I can do, I should do,*
> *and with the help of God,*
> *I will do.*

That friend couldn't find a new job or pay our mortgage for us. He knew that, but he didn't let that helplessness hold him away from us in our difficulty. And what he *did* do has been a living spring of encouragement that has made a real difference to our lives and our faith ever since. And I don't suppose he ever imagined, when he wrote them, that his words would find their way into a book and that the loaves and fishes he gave to us when we were hungry would maybe feed many hundreds of unknown strangers.

The small gesture, expressed out of the deepest reaches of our hearts, can do more than we can hope for or imagine, when it is made in the power of God.

Living water from a hard rock

A natural reaction to reports of devastation and disaster in the world can be the reaction of guilt, that we ourselves are living comfortably and in no imminent danger of being swept away by a typhoon or seeing our country raped and plundered by a murdering army. Others are starving, and we feel guilty about enjoying our dinner. Whole nations face financial ruin, while we worry about the moral dilemma of owning our endowment policies. Such guilt is never productive. But there are other ways of being alongside these overwhelming troubles in the world that are productive and deeply meaningful. I encountered such a way one day during a retreat . . . .

On the face of it the situation was a million miles removed from the devastating events going on at the time in the 'real world', and in Bosnia particularly, which was under heavy bombardment. We were a group of people who had deliberately gone into seclusion for a period of eight days' silent prayer. We broke the solitude and silence only once daily to come together for the Eucharist, during which we were invited to offer our own petitions and intercessions for those we wished to pray for. A hollow gesture?

One day, among the usual prayers for friends who were sick or in need, a new and faltering voice broke through. 'Lord, we remember the people of Bosnia . . . we pray for the children especially . . . the babies and toddlers under bombardment, we bring you their terror . . . their panic . . . Lord, hear us . . . .' And the voice trailed off into brokenness. For a few moments a complete and total silence descended on the chapel. Every one of us was caught up in the heartrending cry to heaven that we had just witnessed. The power of that prayer electrified all who heard it. The man who prayed was with those he prayed for in a way that we couldn't begin to under-stand, but that we recognised beyond doubt.

There was a simple, yet sacred, explanation for the power of his prayer. As a toddler in 1944 he had been in an isolation hospital with scarlet fever, when the hospital was bombed. In his prayer he was expressing the kind of empathy that can only grow from lived experience. His own childhood terrors were being lived out again in his prayer for the Bosnian babies, but it has been transformed into a Calvary prayer that could have come straight from the heart of the Lord: 'Father I *know* where they are. I am where they are. I bring them to *you*.'

I know where they are.
I am where they are.
I bring them to you.

Living out the dream

During the early 1990s a British army officer, serving with the UN peace-keeping forces in Bosnia, was fired by the desire to re-build an orphanage that had been destroyed by shell-fire, and from which the surviving children had been evacuated far away from their home town. The story was re-told in a television programme called *Against the Odds*.

The programme re-enacted scenes from the unfolding drama, beginning with the soldier's enthusiastic, and perhaps rash promise to thirty children that he would give them back their home. Thirty hurting children, who had lost everything in the war and seen their parents slaughtered and their homes destroyed. Their faces lit up in a mixture of hope and disbelief when they heard his promise. They watched and joined in as the men in the officer's command cleared the ruined building ready for reconstruction. And the soldiers in their turn became deeply attached to the children, played football with them, talked to them, began to love them.

The children knew nothing of the terrible struggles being played out behind the scenes to raise the £250,000 needed to fund the project. Nothing of the negotiations with the Bosnian government, the British government, the European Community. Nothing of the countless fund-raising ventures started on their behalf. They had no idea of the cost of their homing, and if they had known, such a figure would have been far beyond the limits of their imaginations.

The site was cleared, but no building had begun. The soldiers were posted elsewhere. They were forced to leave the children behind them, with just their promise, still unfulfilled, and their love. The macho faces of the fighting troops were streaked with tears that day.

The officer, whose dream it had been, gave up his commission, his job, his family life and his reputation. He stayed behind on the site ... because he had promised.

There was hope. There was funding. There was progress. And then the blow fell. The architect announced that the cost would be four times what had been estimated. A million pounds would be needed to complete the project. And the reason was simple: the orphanage, before its destruction, had been a listed building. If it was to be restored at all, it must be restored perfectly. It must become once again the perfect thing its first architect had dreamed it to be. And the cost of perfection was astronomical.

The EU backed off. The Bosnian government stalled. But the bazaars and the car boot sales went on. The project went ahead on blind faith with barely sufficient funds to pay for the initial stages. And, month by month, the pennies in the collecting tins shamed the pounds out of the institutional pockets ....

Until the price was paid in full, the home was restored in its perfection and the broken ones came back to their roots and rediscovered the lost heart of their hoping.

It was a modern parable. A story of destruction redeemed and restored. An exodus in loneliness and terror and a return of the lost ones to the promised land. A challenge to reach for perfection and a cost that stretches us far beyond our farthest limits. Above all it was a parable of covenant love. The love that delivers what it has promised, however high the cost, however impossible the odds.

It leads me to believe that when we 'pray the news' our smallness can *count*, and, like the widow's mite and the car boot sales, become the drop that causes the ocean to overflow. It plants in my heart the truth that when we live out the dream in our own lives, we are living God's dream for creation. When this is our focus, then two column inches can become the space that saves.

TAKING IT FURTHER . . .

Try browsing through your local newspaper, or tuning in to your local radio station. Does anything you read or hear attract your attention especially?

If so, try 'taking it into prayer', but not simply in a straightforward request to God to sort it out. Instead, let yourself spend ten minutes or so in silent, relaxed meditation, imagining yourself to be an active participant in the issue you have been reading or hearing about. Where do you find yourself? What, if anything, do you feel like saying to the other people involved? Listen to anything you think they might be wanting to say to you.

Now let yourself float up in a hot-air balloon. Look down on your own town or village and take a more distanced view of what is going on down there. Gradually, as you float higher, imagine more and more of the world coming into view. How does what is happening in your own small community affect the world around it? Do you notice any connections?

Finally let the balloon take you to God the Father, looking down on the world he has created, seeing all the connections and all the effects of what is happening everywhere. In your prayer now, ask him to place you with his Son. Let Jesus step into the balloon basket with you, and gradually float back down to the earth, back to your own town, back to your own fireside and the newspaper or radio beside you. You are back where you started, but you are not alone in it any more. How do you feel about things now? Is there any way in which you and Jesus together might make a difference?

If you watch the television news in the evening, try to make a habit of noticing one item of news that draws you more than the others. Out of all that you are seeing on the screen, notice one particular face, or one individual person's story. Let yourself be drawn into that story. Try 'walking in the other person's moccasins' for a mile or two. Hold her face in your memory. Later, as you carry this incident or situation to God in your prayer, focus on that single face and that personal story, as if it were happening to your closest friend.

In this way you will, deep in the mystery of things, be walking alongside that person in a way that brings both of you into the unseen presence of God. The comment is made, in the film *Schindler's List* that 'To have saved a single soul is to have saved the world entire'. When you carry one person, caught up in tragedy, in your heart, you carry the whole tragic situation in your heart.

And now the acid test: the person you are carrying is becoming a part of you. Can you do anything at all, however small, to ease the pain she and her people are going through?

An excellent book to help you take this kind of prayer further is *Praying the Kingdom* by Charles Elliott (Darton, Longman and Todd, 1985).

11. A QUIVER FULL OF ARROWS

The habit of instant prayer

A few things stick in our memories for ever, it seems, and one such thing, for me, is what I was taught about prayer as an adolescent in Confirmation classes. One thing especially took root in me at that time, and has never left me, and that was the encouragement to make what were called 'arrow prayers'. Perhaps this way of praying appealed to me then because it was the only method I felt I had the slightest chance of turning into reality in my life. And so, ever since then, I have shot my 'arrows' Godwards at times of special need or concern. Perhaps like many other people, I instinctively shoot off such arrows, for example, every time I hear the siren of an ambulance. Does such 'emergency prayer' have any meaning? Can we weave it into the fabric of our lives? Is it *real*?

Finger-tip prayer

Since the so-called 'Velvet Revolution' of 1989, which freed the then Czechoslovakia from the grip of totalitarianism, the consumer society has moved into Wenceslas Square, in Prague. A vast MacDonalds sign towers over the place of the martyrs. M for MacDonalds. M for Martyrs. A little shrine to the victims of the uprising is marked by a powerful sculpture showing hands reaching up to the heavens out of some unseen, unfathomed pit.

This sculpture reminds me of times in my life and in my prayer when I have reached up to God like that, out of my despair, or my shame, or my need, with just my fingertips reaching above the all-engulfing waves. But it was enough. It was all he needed, to draw me to himself. And it was all they needed too, the martyrs of Prague, to reach out for freedom from the hopelessness of totalitarianism. It was, for them as for me, as expression of a *desire* that was rooted deep in the heart – a desire for freedom, a desire for peace. And desire *is* prayer.

Fingertip prayer. Small signals of need among the tower blocks of daily life. Invoking God's presence in our days – or, more truly, expressing our desire to become *aware* of that constant presence, through the mists of our confusion and our need. Surely such emergency calls reach his ears! But not because he needs to be reminded of his duties towards us like some remote and dispassionate official. Not because he needs *me* to let him know that someone is, even this minute, being rushed to hospital through the streets of my home town.

A familiar scene from family life may come nearer to the truth about what is really happening when we stretch out our fingertips to God in this way . . . . Small children can try our patience to its limits in their stubborn determination to have their own way. Teenagers can do even better, in their adamant refusal to discover the world by any route except their own. Parents who have both these age groups to contend with in one family deserve special commendation. Imagine the scene, therefore . . . .

A family outing perhaps, planned around a picnic in the park. After the first hour or so, boredom sets in. The six-year-old wants to join in a boisterous game with his elder siblings, and gets hurt in the process. There are tears and grazes. A ten-year-old starts to whinge about missing her favourite TV programme and wants to know how long they have to stay in this silly park. And the fourteen-year-old takes himself off without a word and goes missing for a couple of hours. By mid afternoon the family returns, thoroughly depressed, to the pile of breakfast dishes and the prospect of a sullen evening ahead.

But, come bedtime, something changes. The six-year-old unexpectedly flings his arms round his mother's neck, as she tucks him into bed. Nothing is said, but she knows that something has been restored. The ten-year-old slips into the kitchen and does the washing up. Nothing is said, but the signal is understood. The fourteen-year-old summons all his courage and humility together and asks for his father's help with a difficult situation at school that has been troubling him all day. And the parents? Well, maybe they were only waiting to be asked, because until that moment of break-through they knew that the children would resist everything that they might give.

Fingertip prayer can signal just such a moment of breakthrough – a way of telling God, and ourselves, that our resistance has been breached and we acknowledge our need and desire for dialogue with him, and for a restored relationship. Every parent knows the formidable strength of a tiny baby's

*A way of telling God, and ourselves,
that our resistance
has been breached.*

finger. Sufficient power to harness their full-time, undivided attention, and to capture their unconditional love. And so it is with God.

Under the hammer

And I have sat through auction sales too, from time to time, and watched the drama and the delicate sensitivity of the almost wordless interaction between auctioneer and bidder. The language is so muted, barely visible, but the eye is trained and watchful for the slightest indication of intention to buy, and the whole presence of the auctioneer is alert to the merest possibility of interest. It reassures me, when I think of the chemistry of the auction room, that God too will react to my faltering fingertips. He knows when I turn my attention towards him, even when I hardly know it myself.

My fingertip prayer speaks to him more clearly than if I were to stand up in the salesroom and make a huge scene.

I have seen bidders buy mansions with their fingers. I have seen them commit hundreds of thousands of pounds with the slightest inclination of their heads. And I know now, albeit with hindsight, that my silent shafts of longing and of need, and of joy, have always reached the God who first kindled them in me and that his response is out of all proportion to my bid.

Fingertip prayer has sometimes lifted me out of that dark abyss as surely as the flame of resistance lifted the Prague martyrs out of totalitarian control. Not only the martyrs, but their whole nation. And fingertip prayer has also committed me to pay the price of my desires. For we may reach out our fingers in our own need, but when God has responded by drawing us to himself, we ourselves become extensions of his eyes and hands, commissioned to notice the fleeting, wavering movements of others' fingers, and to help him draw them safely home.

I remember especially one arrow that I once shot off to God on behalf of someone else. I realised that this person was desperately seeking help and guidance and encouragement, so I despatched the request to God in the usual way! Very soon afterwards, I was, myself, meditating on the miracle of the feeding of the five thousand. I reached the part where the disciples point out to Jesus that the crowds are hungry and ask him to do something about the situation. To which he replies: 'Feed them yourselves.' These words entered my heart like my own arrow returning to me as a response from God. More like a boomerang really, than an arrow!

Be warned, therefore. When you raise your finger in the auction-room of prayer, you may be committing yourself to pay the market price for your desire — perhaps it is even true to say that God always answers our fingertip prayers, but that we ourselves are not willing to pay the price of those answers. We want the results, but the cheque book remains firmly hidden in our back pockets. And when you fling your arrows at God, they may return to you like boomerangs, pointing out, not always gently, that the help you are begging for someone else may be forthcoming only through *your* action and intervention. No-one ever promised us that prayer would come cheap!

Kingfisher moments

Not all fingertip prayer is about our emergencies. A friend once described her cherished moments of sudden awareness of God's power and his presence as 'kingfisher moments' – like a dart of brilliance streaking across the riverbank, caught for a split second in the full light of the sun. These moments are, truly, occasions of fingertip prayer if we let them become so – this time not the prayer of urgent petition, but the prayer of spontaneous praise.

You may like to share in a couple of my kingfisher moments, and see whether any of your own come to mind . . . .

What a morning it was! A rare and joy-filled morning for a winter-wearied world. I felt resentful that I had to spend it at a desk, buried in a tower block of air-conditioned offices. Yet if I hadn't had to travel into Manchester that morning I would never have had the experience of all that banquet of blossom, birdsong and the overflowing exuberance of spring.

It ought to have been a day for lingering and sauntering, sniffing and savouring, but inevitably I was rushed, and I struggled through the traffic to get myself to work on time. And perhaps, with hindsight, it was good that it was so, because it was precisely because of the speed that I noticed the horse. It was just a split second flash of awareness as I sped by, but it left me thrilling with the glory of the moment. He was standing near the edge of the field, his head raised high, proud yet unselfconscious, above the hedgerow. And the rising sunlight was right behind him, setting him into stark relief against the greens and whites and pinks of grass and blossom.

I passed. And as I passed the sun lit up his head and I saw every bristle on his chin alive with silver, as if transfigured by the touch of eternity. I gasped at the suddenness of the vision, and the words of Jesus' promise drifted through my mind: 'Every hair on your head is counted.' Not only counted, but cherished and valued as if every hair were the *only* hair, and every horse the perfect horse.

It was a resurrection-moment, and it brought my whole day to life. And in all the cart-horse lumbering, blundering days that would follow, I have often returned to this perfect present moment of the silver bristles, and remembered what I knew in that instant, that such times are moments of reality that run through all the mud and the mess and the muddle like a seam of gold.

Another kingfisher moment happened for me one morning on the way home from the school run.

The lights were red at the first junction. I had to wait for a few minutes – it seemed like minutes but I suppose it was only seconds really – at the head of the queue of cars, opposite the house that had always intrigued me. It must have been a child-minder's house, because I would often see small children being delivered there at this time in the morning, and in the summer afternoons there would usually be a crop of youngsters playing in the steeply rising back garden.

I watched the place again that morning, not having much else to occupy my mind until the lights turned green again. There were no children in sight, but a little cat was sitting in solitary splendour on an upstairs window-sill. For a moment I held her gaze, or she held mine! Then she was gone – back to her haunts in the unseen spaces of the unknown house. I had seen her before, very occasionally, when she happened to be sitting on the window-sill at the same moment in time when I happened to be sitting in the traffic queue.

But that morning she reminded me of God. Prayer seems like that. There are moments when we see him, and know his reality in a new kind of way. He shows himself to us when we least expect it. He sits for a moment on our soul's window-sill. And we receive the fleeting gift because we ourselves are also sitting still – usually because of some immobilising circumstances, and the much-resented red lights on our inner journey, that turn out to be graced moments after all.

I recall thinking that I must remember to tell my daughter about the cat that night. But why should she believe me? She would need to see it for herself. If she had seen it, even once, she would *know* that it is truly there, however invisible for most of the time. And we, too, do need the glimpses that God gives us of himself. They are enough to assure us of his permanent reality, however infrequent our 'sightings' of him may be.

The lights turned green again. The moment of eternity was passed and I was back in time again, but I was carrying a new knowledge in my heart, not only of the occupants of the unknown house, but also of the ways of God. There was a knowledge that 'There is a cat living in that house, even though, most of the time, I cannot see it.' The same knowledge as 'God is at home in my heart, whether I think I can see him or not.'

On another occasion, as I well remember, I was on my way to visit a friend on a rather drab estate on the outskirts of a rather drab town. It was 'bin day', and all the wheelie bins were lined up along the roadside. And it was just a day or two before Christmas. It was a rare, crisp, cold, clear morning. As I drove slowly along the road, looking for my friend's house, I was suddenly stopped (literally) in my tracks by the overwhelmingly beautiful vision of a huge cobweb, draped over one of the wheelie bins, and trans-figured by the frost and the sunlight. A kingfisher moment, that gladdened my heart that morning as if in anticipation of the bells on Christmas Eve.

There was never any danger of my forgetting such a moment of glory, but I was reminded of it again several years later, in a group of people who were tentatively beginning to share their experience of prayer with each other. One of them was silent for a long time. When she gathered the courage to share something of the ways in which she felt she had en-countered God during the week, she told us, shyly, how she had been driving to work one cold morning, beneath a grey December sky. Gradually her windscreen had iced up and she had been forced to stop in a lay-by to de-frost it. As she bent to get the scraper from the shelf, she had noticed a small patch of blue sky, letting a streak of sunlight fall to the earth below. And then, she told us, she had noticed the perfect filigree pattern of the frost crystals on her windscreen, and had been left momentarily breathless at their intricate beauty.

The commonplace made holy, and moments of spontaneous joy in us who behold it. Surely the unending song of the angels is the great crescen-do to which our flashes of praise are leading.

TAKING IT FURTHER ...

In a few calm moments, perhaps in your daily 'review' prayer, try to recall any times during the day that you have stretched out the fingers of your heart and thought of God.

Simply notice what those arrows were about. Were they arrows of need or shafts of joy and gratitude? Look closely at any arrows of *need* that you have shot at God today. Bring your need to him now in the stillness of your evening prayer. Ask him to show you any ways in which you yourself can address the needs expressed in your arrow prayer.

- If your arrow was on behalf of someone else, can you do anything to meet that person's needs?
- If your arrow was about your own need, can you now, in the stillness, recognise any ways that may be opening up to you to reach into the roots of the need you have expressed? Arrow prayers are shot off in the heat of the moment, but their answers may most frequently be discovered in the cool of reflection.

The value of arrow prayer may be that it has the power, almost literally, to pinpoint the centre of *particular* needs, either in ourselves or in others. And once the epicentre of the need is recognised, we are much more likely to be open to ways of dealing with those needs, much less resistant to God's action to heal and to nourish. Like the disciples, told to feed the crowds themselves, we may find that God is asking us to be the agents of his miracles in our starving world.

And if you find any arrows of joy in your day, like my moment with the horse, and with the cat at the traffic lights, simply express your gratitude to God for this moment of revelation, when his Spirit bubbled up in you and overflowed into his creation. These moments are life-giving in ways we cannot begin to understand, both for ourselves and for all creation. They are an overflow of God's own creative energy.

12. ZOOMING IN

Going deeper, in the prayer of repetition

Many people come to regard their experience in personal prayer as something very precious to them. For me, prayer is like a goldmine that can lead me to seams of gold deep within my own heart, though it may also bring me up against the hard rock-face of my life's experience as well. The two seem to be inseparable. So I would just like to suggest to you that something so precious is worth exploring more deeply, and to look at a couple of ways that you might like to try, to *deepen* your prayer.

Using the metal detector

We have looked already at the importance of taking time, after a period of prayer, to reflect on what it was suggesting to you about where you are in your journey with God, and how it connects to your lived, day-to-day experience. This period of reflection, or review, can also help you to find the best way to *deepen* that particular line of exploration in your prayer.

If, in your review, you notice any point in the experience that moved you especially, either to a positive *or a negative* response and reaction, go back to exactly that point in your next time of prayer. This may be God's gentle call to you to go deeper into an issue that he wants to explore with you. Make a mental note of any such points, so that you know where to return to next time.

This process is a bit like using a metal detector. You have already established that there is treasure in a particular 'field' (that is, in a particular experience or period of prayer), and now, having sniffed the treasure, you want to dig down more deeply, but you want to dig in the right spot in the field. Or you could compare it to using a Geiger counter to establish the location of an area of high 'radio-activity'.

To use the 'metal detector', or the 'Geiger counter', in prayer, all that is necessary is to still yourself, and then just notice where, exactly, in the prayer, there is a strong reaction in your feelings. At first you may need a little practice to get used to handling the metal detector, but in time you will start to recognise intuitively the point in your prayer that felt the most significant. If the reaction seems to be strong but negative, don't abandon the exercise. A strong reaction is an important pointer for you, even if it feels painful. Trust God to be gentle in his dealings with you. He may dig deep into sensitive areas, but he will do so with tenderness.

The process, of re-visiting significant points in prayer, is often called *repetition*, and you may find that it can continue for many days, focusing on a particular prayer experience, or Gospel passage, as you let your feelings draw you closer and closer to the heart of the matter. Don't try to 'repeat' the whole prayer, as if to get a different slant on it: just stay with that one crucial moment, or conversation that holds you, and ask God for the grace to see what meaning it carries for you.

Renewing old acquaintance

As I write, I have just enjoyed a day in a house where I have often made retreats. Today I was only there for a few hours, and I only had a little time between various meetings, but during those times, I did what I always do when I go back there: I walked along my favourite paths, noticing with renewed joy, places where in the past I have met God in prayer in particular ways, and perhaps with especial power.

Perhaps you have had similar experiences? It doesn't have to be a retreat house of course. Have you ever gone back to a place where you have spent happy times in the past – maybe a holiday resort that holds good memories for you, or a scene of your childhood? You will probably have noticed that, as you seek out your special 'haunts', being back in the familiar places again also brings back the feelings that you experienced at the time. It reinforces the good memories, making them deeper, and renewing your zest and energy for life here and now. How were your feelings during these return visits? Whether good or bad, painful or joyful, these 'repeats' will have reawakened the original feelings you experienced there, and reinforced them, amplifying the energy they are capable of generating in you. For example, the experience of visiting your old home town may stir vivid memories of friends with whom you have lost touch, and those memories may provide the energy boost you need to inspire you to get in touch with an old friend again.

Often a very specific object, or a tune or a smell may bring back whole waves of memory. This is the metal detector effect at work. The sudden discovery of an old toy, or a forgotten letter, a snatch of a song or the scent of hay or of a particular flower or perfume may evoke a huge response in your heart. If you could dig down at that very point in your heart's soil, you would surely find the source of the sudden inner flashover in a cherished relationship or a time of special significance in your life.

So return visits can be life-giving and life-renewing, and return visits to the scenes and events of your prayer can do the same. Try noticing when and where your inner metal detector bleeps most insistently, and ask God to take you deeper.

A particularly fruitful way of re-visiting the places of grace is to make a special point of noticing and treasuring times when you have indeed felt very close to God. These may have been times, perhaps, when imaginative prayer leapt to life for you, or when you felt that you were given sure guidance or new insight in your prayer. Whatever gave rise to such experience, store it in your heart, because it will be a spring of living water for you in times to come.

Remember how we hear in the Gospel that 'Mary treasured all these things and pondered them in her heart' (Luke 2:19). Surely she drew on that store of graced memories when she stood at the foot of the cross. And we do well to draw on her wisdom. When we are close to God we are in 'spiritual consolation'; we are standing in the sunlight of his presence. But the clouds will come down, inevitably. The sun will be no less there, energising us and holding us in being, whether we can see it or not, but the clouds will seduce us into the illusion of being separated from the light of Life. We will be in 'spiritual desolation'. It is during the cloud times that we so deeply need the reassurance of our memories of how it felt when we stood in the sunlight. So treasure your experiences of consolation and store them, like Mary, and ponder them in your heart. They will carry you through the Calvary times. They are part of God's loving provision for your journey through the uncharted pathways of your life.

The diviner's rod

A favourite metaphor of mine is that of the inner compass needle. The compass needle is a way of describing *discernment*, or the gift of discovering the power lines of God's guiding in our lives. It helps us to notice when we are 'living true' to our deep inner sense of 'walking with God', and when other, lesser matters are distracting us from that central purpose and desire.

In Chapter 22 we will look again at the vexed question of why God so often seems not to hear, or at least not to answer, our prayers. Here, we might just stop to consider whether we are really expecting God to wave a magic wand over our life's difficulties and confusion, or whether we might not do better to look for a different kind of rod – the rod of the water diviner?

The 'water diviner's rod' is another metaphor of the process of 'repetition' and it has much in common with the inner compass of discernment. Repetition, or the deepening of prayer in the way we have been exploring, is like searching in the desert for the point where the rod begins to register the unseen presence of water. But the rod we use in repetition is a rod which is sensitive to the presence of the living water that Jesus urged us to seek. This 'divining rod', too, must be held lightly, so that every inner movement of our hearts is registered and noticed. And its tremor must be trusted and acted upon, if the treasure is to be found, just as our discernment compass must be trusted and acted upon if we are to continue on a true course.

'Water divining', in this sense, is much the same as metal detecting. It can be done by following this simple process:

• Move slowly and sensitively across the 'field' of your prayer period.
• Stand still when you register a response.
• Dig down more deeply at that point.
• Keep digging until you strike 'water'.

How do you know when you have dug deep enough? I would suggest that, as in every other way of prayer, you will be able to judge it by its fruits. You will know when you are drawing on the living water because it will release life and energy in you. Receive and absorb this energy and let it inflame your heart and turn your desire into reality. This is what it means to be 'a human being fully alive'.

Digging for rock

If you have ever been involved in building a house you will know how much work goes into the 'footings'. It is essential to dig deep enough to find a solid foundation. This is sometimes no problem, if there is firm ground or rock not too far below the surface. Sometimes the job can become a huge one, exacting great cost in terms of money and energy and time. There is no short cut. If the footings are unstable, the house will fall.

This human experience also helps to lead us into a deeper understanding of what 'repetition' in prayer can mean. Sometimes my own prayer feels (if I look back over it honestly) like building an estate of unstable houses. Day by day I move on, with inordinate haste, from one shaky house to the next, and when the next gale comes the whole estate falls over like a pack of cards. I haven't taken the time or the trouble to excavate the foundations on which I was so recklessly building.

How much more fruitful, for myself and for others, if I had stayed with just the one 'house' and gone down deep enough to make it sure and stable. How much wiser if I had dug down to the rock, before I constructed my own ideas and conclusions over it, like putting the roof on the house before there were walls to support it. How sad God must be, and how frustrated with me, when I lack the patience just to wait and let him show me the deeper roots that underpin my prayer.

And like the house problem, sometimes the foundational truth of our prayer is found fairly easily and obviously. Sometimes it takes much longer to deepen down to 'the heart of the matter.' How can you tell? Well, when we dig for a firm foundation we are looking for stable ground. In prayer we might try testing whether, in any particular issue that is occupying our prayers, we have reached that stable ground. To do this, try carrying what you feel to be the fruits of your prayer on this issue round in your head and your heart through your living of the days. Be conscious of it. Call it to mind. Test it in practice. Will it stand the weight of lived experience? Does it make a difference to how you are? Use your prayer as a touchstone for real decisions and choices.

For example, you may have been praying for guidance in a difficult relationship, and you may have felt in prayer that there was a tug on the metal detector around the place that suggested a particular approach to the 'difficult' person. You may have gone back to that point in prayer, and felt the same kind of tug suggesting itself to you. The repetition may even have opened up a new approach that you hadn't considered before, or modified your attitude in some way. To test whether you have reached 'solid ground' in your prayer over this issue, try calling your prayer to mind deliberately, especially in your dealings with the person in question, or in any matter that concerns the problematic relationship. Test the ground. Put your weight on it. Try to follow the line that suggested itself to you in prayer. Trust that what God has begun he will bring to completion. All he asks of you is a patient obedience to the deepest promptings of your heart.

A question to keep at the forefront of your mind as you dig down like this in the prayer of repetition is this: 'What does this mean for me in practice?' 'Where is the solid core of it, on which I can build specific choices and decisions?'

Not all prayer is about resolving issues like this of course. Frequently repetition is more like sucking a sweet until you have extracted all its flavour, and it has been absorbed into 'who you are'. In your prayer you know that you have come close to God, and your inner Geiger counter will show you where this was happening most significantly. Then, in your prayer of repetition, the deeper truths and meanings of your prayer can be gradually explored. Prayer is like an artist's first broad brush sketch. It captures the fire and the spirit of your encounter with God. But repetition will add all the shades and nuances to that picture, giving it depth and perspective, transforming it (and you!) from God's first sketch into his work of art.

TAKING IT FURTHER . . .

Imagine your prayer as a kind of zoom lens.

- Try focusing this lens on the memory of any moment or period in your life when you felt a powerful sense of God's presence. Stay with the picture that your lens reveals. Just reflect on this memory. Explore the details of what you see through your lens, as it magnifies this moment in your heart. Stay especially with any specific detail of the memory that attracts you, and deepen that detail even further. Respond to God in whatever way feels right for you.
- Now bring back the focus to where you are now. With hindsight, can you see how that graced moment has made a difference to your life? In

Focusing on the place of grace.

what ways? How can you nourish the transformation that this moment began in you?

- Now focus your lens on a past period of your life when you felt trapped in potentially destructive circumstances or relationships. Notice in your prayer the feelings you had then: perhaps restlessness, anger, impatience, frustration, helplessness, despair . . . . Without any judgement, of yourself or of others, simply let these feelings be present to your memory and your prayer.
- Now re-focus again to *today*. You have moved on from that chapter of your story, however you chose to handle it at the time. How has your journey moved since then? Did the destructive circumstances *actually* destroy you, or have you in fact not only survived, but grown, since then? If you have survived and grown, how might this fact affect your

reaction if you should find yourself in 'destructive' times again in the future? How might it affect your response to other people who are going through apparently destructive experiences?

PART THREE

THE WORD MADE PRAYER

In the previous section we looked at some ways of 'focusing the telescope' of prayer. Another very powerful approach to prayer is to focus our hearts specifically on the Word of God as it is revealed to us, whether in his creation, or in the Word of Scripture, or in the words of conversation with him, into which our prayer may draw us.

This section explores some ways of 'praying with the Word':

13. PAGES OF LIFE

Praying with Scripture: an introduction

There is a strange episode recounted by the prophet Ezekiel. He is speaking of his own prayer, and what, with his inner eyes and ears, he saw and heard, as he prayed on one particular occasion. This is how he describes his vision:

> 'I, Ezekiel, heard a voice speaking. It said, 'You, son of man, listen to the words I say . . .. Open your mouth and eat what I am about to give you.' I looked. A hand was there, stretching out to me and holding a scroll. He unrolled it in front of me . . .. He said 'Son of man, eat what is given to you; eat this scroll, then go back and speak to the House of Israel.' I opened my mouth; he gave me the scroll to eat and said, 'Son of man, feed and be satisfied by the scroll I am giving you.' I ate it, and it tasted sweet as honey.
>
> Then he said, "Son of man, go back to the House of Israel and tell them what I have said."'

> (Ezekiel 2:8–3:4)

We could disregard this description as merely a personal flight of imagination on the part of Ezekiel, using rather bizarre imagery at that. But I think that if we do, we may be missing something that is important and universal for us today, especially about how we might pray with Scripture.

Let's just look at the way Ezekiel engages with his vision. First he *hears* the voice of God, and responds to what he hears by *listening*. Then he sees the hand, holding the scroll, and he responds to what he sees by *receiving* what is being offered. Next he *tastes* what has been placed in his mouth, and responds to what he tastes by delighting in its sweetness. And finally he is commissioned to turn what he has experienced into food for the whole people of Israel. These observations highlight at least three ways of being open to God in our prayer:

- We are invited to use our *senses*. Ezekiel receives the revelation from God through his senses of sight, hearing and taste. Opening our five senses to

The Word,
    with a life of its own.

God can bring whole new dimensions to our prayer.

- We are invited to *respond* to what we are receiving. This is a two-way interaction. Prayer is not simply 'down-loaded' onto us, like a page from the Internet. It is the gateway to an interactive relationship, which we may turn into a conversation.

- We are commissioned to turn our prayer into *action*. Like Ezekiel, we are asked to realise that prayer is not given primarily for ourselves, and for our own personal spiritual growth, but for all God's world, and, very specifically, for that bit of God's world in which we 'live and move and have our being'. For Ezekiel this 'bit' was Israel. Where is it for us?

In the beginning is the Word

Ezekiel's prayer vision can take us, if we let it, back to our first beginnings, and beyond. 'In the beginning was the Word, and the Word was with God and the Word was God.' And it can point towards many different ways of praying with that same Word.

That first Word (who is also the final Word, the Alpha and the Omega of all that is), was spoken in creation, expressing himself in every rock and stone, every flower and bird, every star and every slug that was to transform the emptiness of space into a living, teeming universe. And so we discover God, the speaker of the Word, in the many faces of his creation.

Then the Word was spoken in the words of our own languages, in the writings of Scripture and through the mouths of the prophets. God's covenant relationship with his people was unfolded, conversation by conversation, through those who were willing to listen to him in prayer and respond to what they heard.

And when the time was right, the Word became incarnate in Jesus – God's own self, living among us, dying at our hands, and pouring out his Spirit through all the ages still to come. Giving himself as a living sacrifice which we continue to receive in the Eucharist, when, like Ezekiel, we 'take and eat' the living Word, letting him become wholly incorporated into who we are.

Finally, having acknowledged our desire to be at one with the Word in a personal way, in prayer and in sacrament, we ourselves become words of the Word, called to let our lives become expressions of the Word, to speak the Word onwards in what we say and do, and to share it, a living communion, with those who are hungry.

How do we translate these high ideals into real prayer?

In later chapters we will look at some possibilities in more detail, but in summary we might notice several ways in which we can encounter the Word and let that encounter become prayer:

- We can engage with God through his own self-expression in creation. We can 'find him in all things'.
- We can savour the Word as it is given to us in Scripture, by, as it were, tasting it, letting it dissolve in our hearts and fill us with its meaning for us, just as Ezekiel savoured the scroll.
- We can enter into a living encounter with the Jesus of the Gospels, by becoming ourselves, in our imagination, participants in the Gospel scenes.
- We can engage in personal conversation with God in prayer, letting his Word invite our response, talking through with him the things that concern us.
- We can explore the ways in which we are being asked to turn our contemplation into action, for the sake of all God's people.

The Word around us

Sometimes, when I wake up in the morning, or when I take a walk in the woods or the hills, or notice the expressions of the people I meet in the market, I think that God has written his signature in every corner of his creation. Sometimes this signature is obvious, as, for example, in a summer dawn or a silent moonlit night, or the grasp of a new-born baby's fingers. Sometimes we have to search for it among the debris of our dreams. Sometimes God's self-expression in the eyes of his children has been over-laid by the grief and the need and the pain which we have inflicted on each other, and only unconditional love can dissolve that layer of resistance that obscures God's face from us.

Whether easy or arduous, the search is worth the trouble! Those who know St Paul's Cathedral in London will be familiar with the famous epitaph to its architect, Sir Christopher Wren: 'If you are looking for his memorial, look around you.' The same can be said for God, with the one important difference that what we discover of God when we look around us is not his 'memorial' but the signs and traces of his living presence, continually creating all that is.

There are 'clues to the Kingdom' everywhere around us, waiting to be discovered in each day's journeying. Some ways of engaging in this treasure hunt are explored in Chapter 14.

Savouring the Word

When I read about Ezekiel's vision I can almost feel him rolling the scroll around in his mouth and discovering the power of its flavour – surprised, no doubt, that this dry piece of paper should yield such sweetness.

We too, when we hold a Bible in our hands and flick through its thin pages, might be forgiven for wondering how these dry scrolls are ever going to taste sweet! As for taking them into ourselves, 'reading, marking and *inwardly digesting*', as the saying has it, that doesn't sound like a very appealing enterprise at all.

Well there is some good news on this front. There are ways of doing just that, of taking a few words from these dry pages, and savouring them in our hearts until we have extracted the deep secrets of their taste and flavour, and then letting those secrets open up in the ways we live and relate to each other. You might like to look at the suggestions in Chapter 15. And then expect to be surprised!

Living with the Word

It would all have been so different, of course, if we could have actually heard Jesus speak, been present when he healed the sick and raised the dead and called the broken-hearted back into the fullness of life. If we could have eaten and drunk with him, heard him speak on the hillsides, sat in the boat with him and seen for ourselves his laughter, his tears, his toughness and tenderness, then it would be so much easier to follow him with conviction.

Is it really so impossible? We can't put the clock back, but, as we noticed at the beginning of this chapter, we are seeking relationship in prayer with the Word who *is*. Not with someone who merely *was*, or with some perfect state which still lies veiled in the future. We journey with the One who is with us in the present moment, and one way of praying with

Scripture is to enter the scenes of the Gospel (or other places) in our imagination, and let ourselves become, in prayer, a participant in that scene. It is a way of being present to those scenes, and letting them affect us as they might have affected us when they first happened. And it is a most powerful way of entering into an intimate relationship with the Jesus of the Gospels, which may both surprise and transform us in its consequences.

An approach to this form of scriptural prayer is suggested in Chapter 16.

Word and response

Ezekiel may well have been amazed into silence by the encounter with the scroll, but in other places he, and so many other prophets and Old Testament figures, have no hesitation in getting into conversations with God, and, indeed, of giving him the benefit of their opinions, if need be, on how things should be arranged. And I guess most of us do the same, from time to time, especially when God seems to need a hand in getting things right!

So what are our own conversations like? When I look at some of my own prayer-conversations I see something that mainly looks more like monologue than dialogue, and tends not to let the Word get in edgeways. And if I do let God have his say at all, and if I have the grace to listen while he 'speaks', how do I know that it is really God who is speaking in my heart, and not just a kind of play that I have scripted myself?

When we enter prayer, we enter into relationship with God, and relationship leads to dialogue. Some ways of making this dialogue truly two-way, and fruitful, as well as hints for testing its reality and validity, are suggested in Chapter 17.

The Word from the cross

The most agonising Word of God was spoken on Calvary, and continues to be uttered in the pain of his children, being lived out in every corner of his creation through all time. Prayer is hard, when life is hurting. And when we are least able to pray, we need prayer the most.

In Chapter 18 we look at some ways of finding that so-needed prayer when our lives seem to be broken beyond repair.

Word into action

God didn't stop at making himself known through his creation, or through the words of his prophets. When our fallenness had alienated us from his presence, he took our human form and, as it were, rolled up his sleeves and got to work on the mess that we had made out of ourselves, our world and each other. He became the child who taught the Temple elders, the man with the callused hands and the carpenter's apron, and the one who mysteriously breathed his very breath into us and commissioned us to do for each other what he has done for us himself.

If we take this commissioning seriously we must acknowledge, in awe and humility, that we ourselves are being asked to become a channel for making the eternal Word incarnate in our own town, our own generation. We are asked to speak the Word to others in their own language and their own local dialect. And we are being asked to turn the words of our prayer into action for our world, just as the first Word did when he lived among us in human form. A tall order, but when we walk with God we walk tall – tall enough to see the vision beyond the horizon, yet so close to the earth that we can touch the hem of his garment.

This is contemplation in action, and it is explored more fully in Chapter 19.

From words to wordlessness

The more we learn to listen, the more we will realise that what God has to say in our hearts is far more worth listening to than our own barrage of requests and demands on him. And eventually, we will pass from the desire even to listen, into the desire merely to *be* in his presence, enveloped in a life-giving, life-sustaining radiance in which we are all one in him. An approach to this kind of contemplation is explored in Chapter 20.

The river deepens and widens and eventually streams back into the ocean which is both its source and destination. Prayer moves into contemplation. Contemplation opens up into transformation. We have tried to respond to the invitation made to us, as to Ezekiel, to take the Word into ourselves, and in response that same Word takes *us* into *himself* for all eternity.

TAKING IT FURTHER ...

Just notice your own 'gut' reactions to some of the possibilities mentioned in this chapter. How do you feel when you hear it suggested that you might, for example, enter into a two-way conversation with God on a regular basis, or enter the Gospel scenes as if you were really there, so close to Jesus that you could feel the warmth of his breath (or perhaps so far away as to feel alarmed at your own distance from him), or that you yourself are being called to become part of the way in which his Word is becoming incarnate, even now, in his world?

Simply notice your reactions, and maybe make a note of them somewhere. Don't make any kind of judgement on them, and don't try to 'sanitise' your feelings by tuning and tweaking them into what you think is the 'right' reaction. Later, when you have had a chance to go more deeply into some of these forms of prayer, and perhaps tried them out for yourself, come back to these initial reactions and compare them with how you feel then.

Do you have a favourite piece of Scripture? If so, look it up, and maybe write it out on a slip of paper that you can keep with you. The Jews of Jesus' time used to keep Scripture texts in little boxes strapped to their foreheads, to carry the Word with them always in this intimate and personal way. Try carrying your favourite piece of the Word with you in some way and every so often getting it out, reading it slowly, savouring its words, its syllables, its special personal meaning for you. Taste its 'sweetness' and let it become a part of who you are.

14. CLUES TO THE KINGDOM

Finding God in all things

Jesus told us that to have seen him was to have seen the Father. He showed us, again and again, in his own life and personality and ministry, and in the stories he told, something of what God, and God's Kingdom are like. And I would like to suggest to you that *everything* – every creature, every person, every situation – has the power to reveal *something*, however small, of what God is like, if, as Jesus said, we have eyes to see and ears to hear.

St Paul says the same thing in his letter to the Romans:

> *'Ever since the creation of the world, the invisible existence of God and his everlasting power have been clearly seen by the mind's understanding of created things.'*

> (Romans 1:20)

If this is true, it offers us a thrilling challenge ...

Something that you will experience during the course of the coming week will be an important clue for you on your treasure hunt for God. Something will cross your path or catch your attention in some way, which will show you something of the nature and the mystery of God. It may be just a tiny piece in a vast jigsaw, but without it the jigsaw cannot ever be completed. It is up to you to find it and claim it and then to share it with your fellow seekers. Try looking out for that one special moment or incident or feeling which is labelled: *'This is what God is like.'* You could call them *'parable moments'*, and if you were asked to teach other people about God, you could use these parables to show them, in familiar pictures, how you yourself have met him and known him.

Of course, with our mortal eyes, we will probably never see the full picture, but in noticing the pieces that come our way, we will start to look for – and find! – something of God in all things and in *all* situations.

Look out for things that say something to you:

• About what God is like

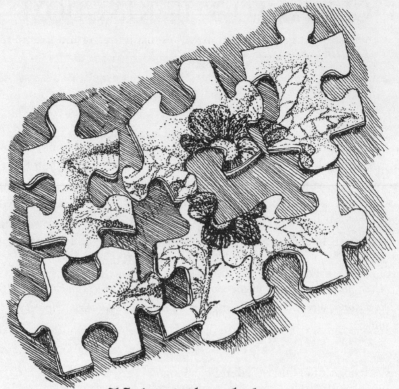

Without the whole,
   your piece has no meaning.
Without your piece,
   the meaning can never be whole.

- About how his Kingdom is
- About how he is asking *you* to be.

   To help you in your search, here are a few examples of places that you might like to look . . ..

In the pavement cracks

For some time after my father's death my mother was quite depressed and turned in on herself. It was a struggle to encourage her to move beyond her understandable preoccupation with her own negative feelings. Then one day she phoned me out of the blue and in the course of that conversation she told me that she had been along to the shops that morning and had noticed a tiny, pink wild rose flowering shyly between two paving stones.

At the time I was overjoyed to hear her obvious delight in noticing this little sign of grace, although neither she nor I would have consciously registered this as a moment of prayer. Yet it was so. I can see that clearly now, with hindsight, and I'm glad to say that she too came to recognise the moment for the gift that it was.

Why was it prayer, rather than just a satisfying moment of observation? Well, I think three things about this encounter suggest that is was a moment given by God:

- The moment with the rose *made a difference* – to her and to me. It had something to say that we needed to hear. It said that the beauty and resilience and determination of life, however vulnerable, will assert themselves over against the hardest resistance and obstruction and will find a way to grow and express themselves.
- The meeting with the rose came at just the moment when she was ready to receive it, and it worked on her in complete harmony with the general pattern of the healing process that was taking place in her. It was *consistent* with all that God was already doing for her and in her.
- Recognising the rose, and its tenacious, exuberant hold on life, left her feeling more at peace with herself, more at one with her inner self and with the created world around her. And this was an effect that didn't fade away, but rather grew stronger as the weeks and months, and even the years passed by. She would remind me of the incident long afterwards and tell me how it had helped to change the course of her desolation.

And so the rose became a kind of icon for her. Whenever she saw a wild rose after that, she remembered that life is truly stronger than death, and gentle perseverance is more powerful than solid resistance. We could say, with truth, that in the little rose she had glimpsed something of what God is like, and of the values that reign in his Kingdom.

In the work-place

I have a colleague whose hobby is wood-turning. He can go to the woodyard and pick up a grimy, weather-beaten lump of timber, hold it in his hands, look at it closely, and then see just what it can be turned into, on his lathe.

He tells me that, as he works the wood, he has to let it 'speak for itself', so that the transforming work becomes a kind of silent conversation between the wood and the wood-worker. Bit by bit the wood reveals its innermost pattern and texture, and as it does so, the wood-turner is continually reflecting on how best to bring out its hidden beauty, and what shape is evolving out of its initial shapelessness. If he is wise, he will let the wood 'co-operate' in its own becoming. The two are partners in the creative act.

My colleague isn't a believer, but when I hear him talk about his hobby, and see the joy in his eyes as he tells me about his latest project, I know that I am seeing a picture of how God deals with us – how he holds the rough, weather-scarred unformed lumps of us in his hands and sees, so deeply, the true reality at the heart of us, only waiting for transformation. And he calls us into a relationship of ongoing co-operation with him as this transformation, this re-creation, is gradually brought about.

In listening to my colleague's thrilled awareness of the potential of what he holds in his hands, I see the joy of God in what *he* sees hidden in the depths of each of *us*.

In the market place

A friend of mine was eager to tell me, the other day, that she had found a picture hanging on a market stall that had appealed to her so much that she felt she really, deeply, desired to buy it and take it home. It was a picture of Jesus, sitting at a well, with two little children beside him. What had appealed to her so much was partly the vague memory of having seen the picture before somewhere when she was a child herself, but mainly the expressions of pure, uncomplicated, unconditional love that the artist had breathed into the faces of the three figures at the well.

The market-seller wanted £16 for the picture. My friend didn't have that much. And anyway, as her husband pointed out, the picture was very dirty and in urgent need of a clean-up and a new frame. In fact you couldn't really see the details, or the beauty of the thing at all, because it was overlaid with grime and dust. They offered £9 for it, and their offer was accepted. My friend walked off with the picture clutched to her chest.

Once home, they cleaned the picture and revarnished the frame, then hung it on their wall. When visitors came, nothing was mentioned, but, again and again, people – not necessarily believers – would stand and gaze at the picture as if they were seeing something dearly loved but long lost and forgotten. There was no need to say anything. My friend simply let the picture speak for itself, and allowed her guests to listen to its meanings for them in their own way.

She knew, as she was telling me about this incident, that she was telling me about the ways of God. About how much he desires us, even when we are unrecognisable beneath the layer of sin and shame that disfigures us. How he comes to the market and will not go home until he has redeemed us. How gently he cleanses and restores us, and places us in the heart of his Father's house. And how he rejoices when other people stop and gaze, and recognise something of our creator's image in us, his creatures.

On the television

Alison Hargreaves, a young climber, lost her life on K2 after reaching the summit. Some months later her widowed husband and two small children went back to K2, to visit the mountain where their mother's body would always remain, for she was never found. This visit was filmed and screened on television.

There was a particularly moving moment in it when the family made a little cairn, where they intended to leave their personal last tributes and gifts to her. When it was ready, her little daughter, Kate, aged four, spoke up and said that, since sweets were her own favourite thing, and she wanted to give her favourite thing to her mummy, she was going to leave a sweet in the cairn.

As she laid her sweet beneath the stones of the cairn I was reminded of our own need to express love and our impotent desire to give to God, and to those we love, what we value most. The picture seems almost ludicrous, at first sight. Our sweets on God's mountain? I pondered these thoughts as I watched the sunrise light up the magnificent profile of K2, where Kate's sacrificial sweet lay. What can our tiny gestures of love possibly mean to God, our Father and the Lord of all creation?

Then my mother's heart felt an unmistakable contraction. I remembered how it feels when your child comes to you, mutely, inarticulately, clutching her most treasured prize, and places it in your hands with upturned gaze and eyes full of pride and joy and a trusting expectation that you will accept and welcome the gift.

Then I knew, not only how Alison Hargreaves felt when her Kate left a sweet for her in the snow, but how God feels, when we bring him our tiny offerings of love and lay them on the broad breast of his love for us. From a television programme about a family of strangers, I had learned what it means to love and to praise the God of Love, and also why Jesus urges us to 'become as little children'.

And in our accidents

I can still remember the day when I broke my driving glasses. One minute they were safely in my hands. The next, they were in pieces on the back door step.

That was the end of my carefully arranged plans for the day. I couldn't drive, therefore I couldn't go to work or do any of the things I had planned to do. I was brought face to face with my complete dependence on something as simple as a pair of glasses. I suppose I had thought of myself, until that day, as an independent working woman, well able to earn my living and look after my family and myself. Those illusions were shattered that morning, along with the glass on the doorstep.

The hassle that ensued to get the problem solved gave me some time to think about my utter dependence on people and gifts that are not mine to claim. I was able to do something about the problem but only because:

- There was an optician in town who had the skill and knowledge to prescribe new glasses for me.
- There were people who could make them, and were willing to exert all their efforts over the next few days to make them quickly, for me, a stranger who had been clumsy and careless.
- I could afford to pay for these services.

It sobered me to think that I am one of a small minority of people for whom these conditions apply. If I had lived in the Third World, or if I were unemployed or destitute in this country, I would just have had to live out my life in the hazy world in which my carelessness had stranded me.

This whole incident showed me something of my relationship with

God, and of my dependence on him. My outward sight, as well as my inward 'vision' are pure gift from God, lent to me for a season, and for a purpose, and not 'mine' at all. And we are gifts to each other, given for a purpose, to love and serve each other. Those few days of sightlessness blessed me with a different kind of insight. God spoke to me through my own carelessness and the apparent misfortune of an everyday accident.

TAKING IT FURTHER ...

I have shared with you some of the ways in which I myself have found the touch and mark of God in my everyday living, in places that I might never have expected to find him.

Of course, God isn't really playing hide-and-seek with us. *He* is there all the time. The problem is that *our* eyes are not yet open to see him. What happens, when we start to look for him in our daily living is that we ourselves become more and more aware of his presence in everything we see and do and are.

We may experience his love, for example, in the neighbour who takes the trouble to ask how we are. Let us remember then that what is done for us by 'the least of his creatures' is done for us by God himself. His is the Love that prompts their kindness to us and ours to them.

Who has brought God's love to you this week?

We may find him in the stories of people we know, or see on television or read about in books or newspapers: stories of patience in the face of suffering, or courage to stand up for justice, or the vision to make changes and inspire others to reach beyond themselves.

Which stories this week have shown you what God is like?

We may hear him speaking to our hearts through our own mistakes and accidents, or even through our own wrong-doing. If we can tune our inner ears to listen, with humility, we will hear his words of encouragement and forgiveness and let him show us to how respond, perhaps by changing our attitudes to ourselves or to other people.

In what ways has God challenged you this week to change in some way?

Creation is a living description of the Creator. It is made in his image. Trees show us how to thrust our roots down deep and not stay with shallowness. The stars teach us that some things can only be glimpsed through the dark parts of our lives. Our family pet can help us see what it means to trust the one who loves you.

What has God taught you about himself this week through one of his creatures?

Often, like children in school, we learn most from our mistakes and the things we spoil. The things that go wrong sometimes have the effect of pulling away some of the false certainty that makes us rely on ourselves, rather than on God. In our apparent failures, we begin to see ourselves in a more truthful light, and are a little less likely to be taken in by our own disguises. We remember that the victory of our redemption was won in a place of shame and apparently total failure.

What has gone wrong for you this week, and has it shown you anything of God's ways of working in your life?

If you feel able to do so, choose a clue, or a 'jigsaw piece' from your week's experience and share that special insight that God has given you, with a friend you can trust, so that all his people may be helped and encouraged to grow in our understanding of him and of his Kingdom.

A fascinating approach to finding God in the midst of family life and helping children to pray is Helen Albans' book *Praying with Sticky Fingers*. It is published by the Methodist Church and available from the Methodist Publishing House, 20 Ivatt Way, Peterborough, PE3 7PG.

15. OUT OF THE CHOCOLATE BOX

Discovering 'lectio divina'

As children we were taught not to take the nicest chocolate biscuits or the biggest strawberries, but the prayer I have called 'chocolate box prayer' invites us to do exactly that. God takes us to a well-spread table and says: 'From all that you see, take what you most desire!'

Like the action-replay prayer we have explored, and like the imaginative prayer that we will look at in Chapter 16, 'chocolate box prayer' is also a way of prayer that has been used traditionally through countless generations and is known, in 'textbook terms' as *lectio divina*. Let me explain how it first began . . ..

A lesson from the monks

Back in the times of the earliest monasteries, when almost no-one was able to read, not even most of the monks, the brothers found an ingenious way of combining the daily Scripture reading with their own personal prayer, in a way that we can use just as effectively today in our very different world. The 'feast' that was set before them in this way of prayer was the daily reading, and it was served by the monk who could read. It was served slowly, with plenty of time for everyone to savour its taste.

As the listeners savoured this 'feast of words', they were invited to choose any part of it that especially appealed to them, and, literally, to take it away, in their minds and hearts, and chew it over in their cells. The phrase or words each one had chosen then became the focus for his private prayer and meditation. They became the focus point for his 'telescope' that day.

Usually the day's Scripture would be read, and re-read, several times, and one by one the monks would disappear, having found their 'favourite chocolate', and would carry off their treasure to the privacy of their own

Browsing the brochure,
then living the reality.

cells, to discover what it had to tell them. Until eventually there was no-
one left, and the reader could go to his own prayer.

Smorgasbord at the Dinorben Arms

There is a pub in North Wales called the Dinorben Arms, which always
makes me think of this way of prayer. They serve a 'help yourself to whatever you want' lunch, and there is a notice over the food servery inviting
people to try a bit of everything and then come back for more of what
they most enjoy. And this is quite a good way of looking at 'chocolate box
prayer'. We read, or listen to, a piece of Scripture, and 'try' each word, each
phrase, as they slowly pass before us, and when we find a phrase, or a
thought, an image or a memory, or whatever moves us in some way, we
stay just there, and let that become our prayer.

You could compare it to browsing through a holiday brochure, and
letting your attention settle on a place that somehow appeals to you. You
see the picture, perhaps, and read the details, and something about that

particular holiday attracts you. You might make a note of it, and show it to your family. Together you might decide to give it a try, and book a week at the resort. *Then* you will find out just what promise it held for you, and whether that promise is fulfilled in reality. Your instinctive feeling about the place is tested out by really *living out* the experience of being there. In 'chocolate box prayer', hearing or reading the Scripture passage is like browsing the brochure, choosing your phrase or sentence is like choosing your holiday, and taking that phrase into your personal prayer is like actually experiencing the holiday as a part of your life.

There is no need at this stage to ask why this particular phrase is speaking to you, or to try to analyse your reaction – in fact to do so would be a distraction, and an effort of the head instead of a response of the heart. What is actually happening is that your subconscious mind is 'registering an interest' in this word or image before your conscious mind has had a chance to get in the way. Like a buyer at an auction sale, your subconscious mind, guided by the Holy Spirit, raises a finger, as it were, to say: 'I'll have that please.' It is the same kind of response that you might feel spontaneously when looking at a sunset, for example. You might simply want for nothing more than to gaze, and to appreciate, and to let the beauty soak down into your being. You are truly 'listening with your heart.'

This kind of deep listening automatically leads you to reflect on your experience, and to respond to it, in ways which will live on long after the time of prayer itself is over. In fact these responses to God's word heard deep in your heart will quietly change your whole way of being, as surely as the water of Cana was silently, invisibly, turned into the finest wine.

After the auction

When you have chosen your phrase, or 'bought' your treasure at this auction, simply savour it, roll it around in your mind and heart. Let God reveal its particular mystery for you. And then take it home, right back into your lived daily experience.

Where and how does it connect to the lived reality of your everyday life? How does it fit into your 'real world'? Trust that God will speak to you in some personal way through that word, phrase or image. You may, for example, find yourself remembering a time when you have had similar feelings to those the phrase evokes in you. Just notice these feelings, whether of delight or of pain. Perhaps the phrase will challenge you, or affirm you, question you or comfort you in some way. Simply notice what is happening inside you and receive it as a gift from the Lord.

And so, your phrase has become a gateway to a conversation with the Lord. Tell him, in your prayer, about the feelings that have been roused in you. Tell him about any memories, any hopes or fears that you have become aware of. Ask him, quite simply, as a child might ask a parent, to show you what he wants to show you through this prayer, and let yourself simply rest in trustful open-ness to his response.

Bring your prayer to a close by thanking him for the gifts he is bestowing deep in your heart, in ways that lie beyond your knowledge or imagination. And, as with any kind of personal prayer, it is good to reflect afterwards, perhaps with a trusted friend, on what, exactly, held your attention so strongly, and why. This is a way of going down to the deep roots of your responses, where you will come closer to the real sources of your joy and your pain.

Of course, when you tell God about your feelings, your memories, your hopes and dreams and fears, (whatever method of prayer you are using) you are only telling him what he already knows, because he is closer to you than you are to yourself. But the reason for doing this is not to 'tell' God, but actually to tell *yourself*. When you are able to say in prayer, for example: 'I feel a sense of fear and foreboding about something that is being asked of me right now', you are (quite possibly for the first time) bringing these fears into the conscious part of your mind, where they can be dealt with much more easily.

If you can take this further and, in your reflection, start to recognise, for example, that these fears that you feel today are actually coming from times maybe far back in childhood, when your confidence may have been undermined by relentless criticism, then you will have moved even further down the track towards letting God heal these damaged places in your heart. In the same way, if you can acknowledge, for example, that something in your prayer is activating a feeling of unexpected joy in you, and if you can go 'ten feet down' to look for the root causes of this joy, you may find that some cherished, but buried memory lies at the heart of it. This might be God's way of getting you back 'in touch' with buried parts of your experience that have been – and still are – sources of energy and life for you.

And the great thing is that taking the biggest chocolate in the box doesn't deprive anyone else of *their* favourite! Far from being a selfish activity, the prayer that takes you deeper into yourself, is also taking you more deeply into a communion where we are, truly 'all one'. What is healed in *you* is healed, in some mysterious way, for *all* the human family, and what releases joy in you increases the joy of all.

Packed lunch prayer

Perhaps I might share with you a particular way in which the prayer of 'lectio divina' can provide a 'quick snack' in a busy day.

It was during the school holidays, and we had visitors staying. Work was pressing and my quiet space seemed quite inaccessible. I was missing the time of quiet in the early morning, yet there seemed no chance at all to carve out the space and solitude from between the demands of those around me. One morning I was longing for a return to the known routine, but it looked like just another struggle for space and time. Eventually, however, I snatched a sacred five minutes on my own in a quiet corner. It was just long enough to ask God for the grace of peace and light and to read the daily readings. Nothing more.

A line in the psalm held my attention:

> '*Sons shall be yours in place of your fathers.*'
>
> (Psalm 44)

There was no time to meditate on it, but I knew that it was speaking to me about freedom from baggage inherited from the past, and fruitfulness in an unknown future. Freedom and fruitfulness. I seized the crust of prayer gratefully, and as I did so I could hear God speaking somewhere inside me:

'Packed lunch prayer today, to keep you going through a busy day. Have a nibble, a snack, a "biting-on", whenever you feel soul-hungry. Take this phrase out and feed on it whenever you have a moment's peace.'

And I knew that I had been given food for the day's journey – not a three-course meal but a nourishing packed lunch.

You can use this approach to prayer using any passage that attracts and draws you. You can also use other, non-scriptural material (such as poems) in the same way, or you can let a visual image or painting speak its personal meanings to you by noticing the details that draw your special attention, and then taking them into prayer. In 'chocolate box prayer' we simply trust that God will speak to us, whatever raw materials we use to focus our hearts upon him. God, the Creator, can and does use any and every part of his creation, to speak to the hearts of his creatures.

TAKING IT FURTHER ...

Using one of the stillness exercises we have been practising – or any other way of coming to stillness that you feel comfortable with – relax and ask God for the gift of prayer. Ask him to open your heart to the personal meaning that the words you will read hold for you in some way.

Then read a passage of Scripture (maybe the daily reading, or any passage that appeals to you or draws your attention), slowly and reflectively, noticing every word, every phrase, every sentence. If any word or phrase seems to hold your attention, or triggers feelings in you, either negative or positive, just notice it and store it away in your memory.

Now re-read the passage, still slowly and searchingly. If the same word or phrase catches your attention, stop your reading and try to sink into prayer, taking your phrase with you. Otherwise, keep on reading and re-reading the passage, until you find your 'chocolate'.

Once you have 'your' phrase, just let it hover there in your prayer, connecting you to God. From now on your phrase will be your prayer guide and director. Just notice whatever memories, feelings or scenes that it evokes in you. These are images and promptings rising into consciousness from your own hidden depths, called up by the word of God that you have chosen. Just let them come up, unrestricted, unrepressed.

Do these memories, images or feelings connect to anything that is happening in your life at present? If so, you might like to let your prayer become a conversation with the Lord. Tell him just how you are feeling. Re-live the memories with him alongside you. Express your joy, or your anger or frustration, your confusion, your uncertainties. Don't be afraid, if the passage opens up doubts in your mind, to say: 'But Lord, it isn't like that for *me*!'

Expressing a doubt in this way is often a first step to reaching a deeper, and more mature layer of trust that may lie underneath it – like scraping away the loose sand to reveal the solid rock below. Or it may be a way of clearing your mind of issues that seem to be clouding your vision but are in fact not important to your deeper quest for God. No-one can predict where prayer that is personal encounter with God may lead. But we can *trust*. The journey of prayer is a journey of trust, and trust will lead to discovery.

A very helpful book for exploring this approach to prayer is:
Too Deep for Words – Rediscovering Lectio Divina by Thelma Hall (Paulist Press, 1988)

16. JUST IMAGINE . . .

Meditating the Gospels imaginatively

Imagination and prayer? Surely they go together like oil and water! This might well be your first reaction to the suggestion that imagination has any place in a Christian's life of prayer. And your second reaction might be: 'Anyway, I don't have any imagination.'

Let's deal with the second objection first. Have you ever waved good-bye to a loved one at a railway station – perhaps seen your son or daughter off to college, or taken leave of your grandchildren after a half-term holiday or taken a friend to the airport – and then, for days afterwards perhaps, found yourself wondering what they would be doing right now, and imagining their new surroundings? Or have you ever come home from a particularly memorable holiday, and, after your return, kept thinking back to the place and the people you had come to love, and imagining what you might be doing if you were there again?

If you can answer 'Yes' to any of these suggestions, then, at the very least, you cannot claim not to have any imagination. And, more than that, you know how to use it to *re-connect* yourself to people and places that you have loved but that are at present out of physical reach.

And if you still think you don't have any imagination, just shut your eyes for a moment and think of the sound of a piece of chalk scratching across a classroom blackboard. Did you find yourself wincing inwardly? Did your memory fly back briefly to your schooldays? Or, more recently, perhaps, can you bring to mind the sickening thud of two cars in collision? If so, what feelings does that memory evoke in you?

Rarely, if ever, does a person really have 'no imagination'. And we use our imaginations in all kinds of ways, that we are probably unaware of. For now let us just go back to that kind of imagining that we might do after a memorable holiday – the kind of imagining that re-connects us to people and places we have come to love . . . .

Because this kind of imagining can become a gateway to prayer! If we can connect ourselves inwardly to other people and places, we can use the same approach to become 'connected' in a special, and conscious, way to Jesus and to his earthly living, dying and rising. Jesus the man, who lived in Palestine two thousand years ago, is physically 'out of reach'. But our imaginations, used alongside the Gospels, can draw us into a personal encounter with as much power to change and transform us, as it did for the friends who accompanied the human Jesus all those centuries ago.

The only way to test this out is to try it for yourself. If you find it helpful, it may become a powerful way of prayer for you. But, like every other approach, it is only one way to pray, and not *the* way.

Where two worlds meet

It would all be so different, so much simpler, if we could have been there when Jesus lived on earth. We began our venture into ways of praying the Word with these thoughts (in Chapter 13). And we recalled that Jesus is *present* (not past or future) to us. Imaginative prayer takes hold of both these facts:

- It *is* amazingly powerful to be present to the Lord in the events of the Gospels, and
- He *is* present to us where we are in our daily lives.

Your imagination can become the place where these two worlds meet: the world of Gospel reality and the world of your daily life.

All you need to do to begin to pray in this way is to choose a Gospel story that especially appeals to you (one of the healing miracles for example). There is no need to agonise over which passage to choose. God will speak to your heart, whichever passage you choose. Begin, as always, by asking God to be your guide and to give you the gift of prayer, and trust that whatever your imagination brings up will be enlightened by the gift of the Holy Spirit. Now simply relax, maybe close your eyes or focus on some steady object such as a candle or a flower, and let yourself just imagine what the scene is like.

This is a very passive kind of exercise. Try not to let yourself be seduced into the need for effort. This isn't a test of your powers of descriptive writing or painting. It is simply the completely passive state of *letting yourself notice the pictures in your mind*. The scene that may suggest itself to you may appear to have nothing remotely to do with the Palestine of 2000 years ago. This doesn't matter. What matters is what your unconscious mind is offering up for your attention. Just notice the scene, without attempting to 'stage manage' it.

You may like to use some of these questions as a framework for your exploration of the scene you have chosen:

- What can you see, hear, smell, taste, feel?
- What is the weather like? Warm, cold, windy, peaceful, wet, dry?
- What seems to be happening in the scene? Who is there? Anyone you recognise?
- What kind of 'atmosphere' does the scene suggest? Inviting, threatening, vibrant, solemn?
- Does any particular part of the scene attract your attention more than the remainder?

Entering the action

So far you have 'set the scene'. Whatever is there has arrived via your own imagination, under the guidance of God, in whom your prayer is firmly rooted.

You might compare this process with the way you look at the opening scene of a play. The curtain rises, and a scene is revealed in which the action will begin to happen. In the theatre, or the cinema, you know nothing, as yet, of how that action will work itself out, or what the characters will be like. And this is how it is, too, at the beginning of your imaginative prayer. You have read the script, certainly, and you are perhaps even over-familiar with the events of the Gospel passage you have chosen, but what about *your* part in it? Powerful drama has the effect of drawing the audience into its own life, and of *changing* the way they see and feel things in the future. And as Christians we believe that the Gospel is the most powerful drama there is. Will it stay on the pages of your Bible, or will you risk entering the action?

To enter into the Gospel in your prayer is indeed a leap of faith, because, however familiar you may be with the stories on which you are focusing your prayer, you cannot begin to predict what will happen when you get up from your comfortable front stall seat in that 'theatre', and walk onto the stage. Then the whole perspective changes. Suddenly you have a role in the drama. Simply by being there, you have become part of the action. You have stepped into the *present moment* of the drama, and you have surrendered the security of knowing the beginning, middle and end of it. You are in the middle of it yourself, and it is happening around you.

When you reach this stage of your imaginative prayer, you might find this kind of question helpful:

- Where do you find yourself? Perhaps you are one of the crowd, or one of the disciples? Perhaps you feel like an outsider looking in, or perhaps you identify with the person being healed or challenged, or invited into a new relationship with Jesus? Don't make any judgements, or try to force yourself to be where you think you *ought* to be. The power of this kind of prayer is in being where you really find yourself, and letting the Gospel light shine on that place.
- How are you feeling about what is happening in your scene? Disturbed? Attracted? Curious? Afraid? Eager?
- Do you feel drawn to speak with anyone there? What do you feel you want to say? What do you feel is being said to you? Can you enter into a conversation with Jesus?
- If you noticed, earlier, that one part of the scene drew you more power-fully than any other, let yourself follow that drawing now. In your imagination, go to that part of the scene. Without forcing anything against your inclination, just see what it is in that part of the scene that is attracting you.

If you feel able to do so, end your prayer by entering into a conversation (see Chapter 17) with Jesus, or perhaps with one of the disciples, or with Mary. Just express your feelings about the experience, and let your heart be open to receive whatever God may want to suggest to you. When you are ready, close your prayer in whatever way you find most helpful, and spend a few minutes in reflection (see Chapter 4).

How do I know this is prayer?

We cannot by-pass the question with which this chapter began: Can my own imagination have any valid place in my prayer? Most of us tend to distrust our imagination. We regard it as the stuff of fairy-tales, not to be indulged beyond childhood, when real and serious living takes over. We suspect it of being only one step short of deception. Our children tell us of some great dream they cherish in their hearts, or of some terror that haunts them, and we dismiss it with the words: 'You're only imagining it.' Or perhaps we confide in a friend some deep desire, only to have it shrugged off with a smiling 'Dream on!' Yet the longer I live, the more I become convinced that my imagination is a God-given gateway to prayer, a place where I meet God in ways that my busy conscious mind cannot interfere with.

When I think of my own relationship with my imagination, I see an ocean, with boats busily plying to and fro, running my life's errands and trading for my bread and butter. How easily I can stay up there on the surface of myself, managing the traffic of my boats and forming alliances with the islands and continents that I can see around me. But if I do ever stop to wonder what is in the depths beneath me I might feel drawn to put on a diving suit and go and have a look. I might find a whole new, undiscovered world down there. There may be sharks, but there will be shoals of exquisitely beautiful fish as well. The imagination is like that underwater world. It can take us below our normal conscious functioning and show us something of the desires we may not even realise we have.

It reminds me of the day when Jesus and Peter were confronted by the tax-man, demanding to know whether they were required to pay the local tax. Jesus sent Peter to catch a fish from the lake and look into its mouth, where he would find the necessary coin to pay the tax for both of them. Imaginative prayer sometimes feels like that for me. I meet the Lord in the Gospel, and he tells me, as it were, to go down into the images I find in the ocean of my own imagination. He invites me to take hold of these images, just as they come, as Peter caught hold of the first fish that swam past. If I look into these images, or into my own imagined reactions to a particular Gospel scene, I will find a 'coin' of their meaning for me. This coin may become the key to a new layer of understanding of myself and of my own, and God's, desire for my onward journey.

Perhaps I might share with you one of the 'coins' I once discovered inside a fish of my imagination's prayer, to illustrate how the Gospel story can connect vividly and fruitfully with our own experience and memory. The scene of this particular prayer was the wedding at Cana (John 2:1–12) ....

I had been to Cana before, and now, as then, I felt oddly out of place there. I couldn't find the right kind of contact with the party-goers. I suppose I just wasn't in a party mood. It was a hot summer day. Everybody was outside in the field. Most people were sitting at the tables, eating and drinking. I suddenly felt very shy and lonely. I was standing quite close to you and your disciples. It felt a bit safer like that. So I could easily hear what passed between you and your mother. 'They've run out of wine', she said, in a matter-of-fact tone. It seemed obvious to her that you could solve the problem.

You had been enjoying the festivities, and I could see that the unexpected challenge upset you. You were quite sharp with her. It was as though you had come to an abrupt turning point in your life and it had shaken the ground beneath you. It had taken the course of future events out of your control. I felt disturbed by the incident, but I could identify with you in it very strongly. It seemed to reflect a sense of disorientation that I was aware of at the moment in my own life.

Were you reading my thoughts? What made you come over to me in the way you did, I wonder? 'There has been a running out for you, too, hasn't there?' you asked me, quietly, so that no-one else could hear. I nodded, surprised that you should be able to see inside me so clearly. 'Come with me', you said. 'I know the emptiness. I understand the hesitation.' I followed you as you walked, pensively, a little further away from the party crowd. I let you walk ahead. You needed space for yourself, I could see that. Mary walked beside me, in an un-obtrusive sort of way. 'Don't worry', she reassured me. 'Just do as he tells you.'

We passed by the six stone water jars. I barely noticed them. The servants were filling them up with water from the nearby well, but it was an everyday scene. No surprises there. You stopped one of the servants and told him to draw off a carafe of water from one of the jars and take it over to the host. I noticed the rich crimson wine running into the carafe. I don't think I had ever seen such a richly coloured wine before, but even then the nature of what had happened didn't really sink in.

You sat down on a boulder at the edge of the field and beckoned me to join you. We sat there together in silence for a while. I closed my eyes against the dazzling sunlight and let my thoughts trickle away into the grass, like water draining away from an overturned pitcher. Eventually I had emptied myself into the silence that enclosed us. The old had passed painfully away and was gone. I felt drained in every way, and sad for the emptying. Yet there was a cleansing in the empty space. It had been a necessary emptying. What had been there could not have stayed longer. It had been time for birth.

I thought of my own child's birth. I remembered that strange vacuum I had experienced when what I had carried was no longer in me. The sense of a dramatic passage from an old to a new creation. I remembered the complete exhaustion that followed, and I felt something of the same exhaustion there beside you on the rock, in the afternoon heat. I had sweated then, too, and the midwife had moved the fan closer to my forehead. Now a gentle breeze brushed my brow and I knew it had to do with you. You were assisting at a birth, yet not a word was spoken.

And there was another birth, a re-birth of spirit when, during my darkest, bleakest weeks you had suddenly, without reason, warning or deserving, filled me with a new and overwhelming sense of your presence and your love. It had felt like a tiny stream turned overnight into a fast-flowing torrent, bursting its banks and overflowing with the joy of being close to you. The mystery of that unexpected cascade of living water remains your secret, but it filled my six stone jars to the brim, in readiness for whatever transforming action was to come.

My memories returned to the labour ward and slid softly through the first hours of the baby's life. With vivid recollection I experienced again that tingling sensation that signalled that my body was ready to feed its firstborn. I looked up at you, and you were gazing steadily into my face. I heard again your words to the servant: 'Draw off a carafe of water and take it to the guests.' But this time the words thrilled me with the full sense of miracle. With a surge of love I took my daughter in my arms, and with her tiny mouth she drew her first nourishment from me. My drained, exhausted, empty body of yesterday had become a source of life and growth for the newborn. I had done nothing, felt nothing, yet overnight an amazing transformation had occurred, and the life-giving milk flowed out of emptiness.

That had been many years ago now, but there in the sunlit field it had returned to me as if I were re-living it. I moved closer to you, to thank you, to kneel before you in recognition of who you are. You stroked my bowed head. 'And so it is with the water of your soul', you whispered softly. 'You didn't do anything. You didn't notice anything. But in the silence and the emptiness, your creator was making all things new. At first the transformation remains a secret. The water jar does not know what it contains and the world cannot guess. But the day comes, for you too, when I invite someone to draw from you a carafe of needed refreshment, and the expected water is found to be the finest wine. The miracle is only recognised when the wine is drawn. If it stays in the jar, it might just as well be water, but if it is drawn off and shared, it will bring joy and the fullness of life.'

We walked back across the field together, side by side, in comfortable companionship, and I understood the heart of the feasting and rejoiced in the richness of the promised vintage.

We began by considering the need to 'focus' our hearts towards God in some particular way. The way of imaginative prayer is one way of practising this 'focusing', but it does more than that: it draws together two different, but connected 'stories' – the Gospel story you are imagining, and your own personal story. This has the effect of bringing the two into a single focus, so that the Gospel light, and the light of Jesus' living presence really does shine upon your own lived experience in very specific detail. The results of this focusing may challenge you to the core, but they will also bring you joy, a new depth of friendship with God and a fuller understanding of what it might mean for you to become ever more fully alive in Him.

And how do I know (for example in the prayer encounter I have described), that this was prayer and not just a day-dream? I would suggest these ways of testing your prayer experience and discerning what is of God and what is merely a passing fantasy:

• What comes from God will last, and will bring about real change within you. The 'Cana prayer' is well over six years old now, but I remember it as vividly as if it were yesterday, and it has become part of who I am. It has changed my perspective on things, especially when I am feeling 'drained', and it continues to give me a vision of the power that is released when we are 'poured out'.

• What comes from God has a peculiar characteristic of weaving itself, seamlessly, into our own very personal experience and our memories. In the 'Cana prayer' you can almost feel the Lord's fingers picking up the threads of my feelings of desolation, and my memories of childbirth, and folding them into his own experience of challenge and hesitation when the wine ran out at Cana. There is a deep consistency, in authentic imaginative prayer, between our own experience and God's self-revelation. There is a kind of oneness between the way he reveals himself in the Gospel narrative and the way he reveals himself through the windows of our memory and the images that arise from our sub-conscious minds. It can feel almost like reading a parallel text translation of an ancient classic. We read the original text in the pages of the Gospel, and alongside it, intertwined with it, we read our own memories and experience.

• What comes from God will always tend to draw us closer to him and closer to each other, though it may lead us through hard challenges. What comes only from ourselves will tend to focus on ourselves, and therefore lead us further away from God and from each other. An encounter with God leaves us with an awareness of a movement towards life and growth, which self-focused pondering can never yield.

Some questions, then, to ask yourself:

• Has my prayer made any difference to the way I am?
• Is my prayer consistent with what is happening in my life?
• Does my prayer lead me closer to God and to other people, or further away?
• Where is the centre of gravity: in me, or beyond myself in God and in his creation?

If you can answer these questions positively, then you can be assured that your prayer was more than just a flight of fantasy. If there are good fruits, then they can only have come from a sound tree. All you need to do is to give that tree the time and space to grow in your heart, and allow the fruits time to ripen.

All through this chapter we have concentrated mainly on the use of imagination to enter the Gospel scenes. Your imagination can, however, be used very powerfully on any piece of Scripture, or, indeed, you may find it helpful to pray imaginatively with non-scriptural material. Many people find that a piece of poetry, or a picture can open up unconscious streams within them and lead them into the communion of prayer. Others discover a key to their inner world in fantasy prayer, simply by allowing an image (perhaps of a tree, or a remembered scene) to form freely in their mind and following in prayer wherever it leads them.

And if you are one of those people who remember their dreams you have another rich vein of treasure accessible to you. Notice your dreams, especially what some people call 'big dreams' – the kind of dream that stays with you long after you dreamed it. I personally have often found that dreams like these have helped me to become aware of hitherto unrecognised areas and layers of my being. Such dreams have become a kind of ongoing prayer within me and have continued to release guiding and transforming power.

My light or God's? An exercise in discernment

Prayer brings light. Jesus said he was the 'Light of the world', and this is the Light we seek in prayer. How do we know, when we think that there has been enlightenment in our prayer, that the light is really of God, and not merely our own?

Discernment might be helped by the following guidelines:

• The light that comes from God makes a difference. It is like light from the sun: it generates and sustains life; it keeps us warm; it makes us grow; it provides energy that we can feel, and trust, and use. When we follow it, we *know* that we are being enlivened.

• Our own lights – our intellectual sparks and bright ideas may dazzle, but they will not leave us with this inner warmth and they will not bring about any true growth or change in us. In their effects, our own lights remain cold, and without miracle-powers

My own 'lights', I find, may momentarily illuminate a part of my tangle of experience, but they will fade, as soon as my battery runs low. God's Light enlivens all creation. It sustains us and forms us, even as we grope around in our darkness with our pocket torches.

TAKING IT FURTHER ...

Relax and use whatever method helps you to come to inner stillness. You are sinking 'ten feet down'. You are bringing the dish of your 'telescope' to stillness, to await the gift of prayer . . . .

An experiment in imaginative prayer

Try to imagine a scene that happened just a short time before Jesus entered into the final, terrible week of his life. He is visiting friends in Bethany, not far from Jerusalem – Martha, Mary and Lazarus, together with some of his disciples, including Judas. Not long previously he had raised Lazarus from the dead, and this had attracted the attention of the authorities. Lazarus' journey back to life had become the immediate cause of Jesus himself being sentenced to death. Perhaps, as they share this meal together, the four friends are somehow aware of these connections – of the joy at Lazarus' return to life, of the sense of wonder at the power in the hands and the heart of their friend Jesus, and of a vague apprehension, a dull fear of the darkness looming ahead of them, that had not yet shown itself, except as a dim sense of dire threat.

Before you begin your prayer, read through the passage where this scene is described. You may feel drawn to read it through several times, letting

Groping through my own tangles,
or seeing with the Light of the World?

the 'feel' of it sink into you. Read slowly, as if soaking up the atmosphere of the place, and the feelings of the people.

> *Six days before the Passover, Jesus went to Bethany, where Lazarus was, whom he had raised from the dead. They gave a dinner for him there; Martha waited on them and Lazarus was among those at table. Mary brought in a pound of very costly ointment, pure nard, and with it anointed the feet of Jesus, wiping them with her hair; the house was filled with the scent of the ointment.*
>
> *Then Judas Iscariot – one of the disciples, the man who was to betray him – said, 'Why was this ointment not sold for three hundred denarii and the money given to the poor?' He said this, not because he cared about the poor, but because he was a thief; he was in charge of the common fund and used to help himself to the contents. So Jesus said, 'Leave her alone; let her keep it for the day of my burial. You have the poor with you always, you will not always have me.'*
>
> *Meanwhile a large number of Jews heard that he was there and came not only on account of Jesus but also to see Lazarus whom he had raised from the dead. Then the chief priests decided to kill Lazarus as well, since it was on his account that many of the Jews were leaving them and believing in Jesus.*
>
> (John 12:1–11)

Imagine the place where this scene is happening. How does the room look, and feel? Notice the details that come to mind – the shape and size of the room, the furniture, windows, views out of those windows

Who is in the room? Where are *you*?

Take time to notice everything that makes the place how it is: see the colours, listen to the sounds you can hear – the sounds outside the house, and the sounds inside. Notice any scents – perhaps the smell of cooking or the fragrance of flowers. Use all your senses to re-create the scene as feels 'right' for you.

How do you *feel* in that scene – comfortable, peaceful, disturbed? Don't make any judgements or try to work out reasons for your feelings. Just let them be there and become aware of them.

Now turn your attention to the *people* in the scene. What are they doing? Are any conversations taking place? How is the underlying mood of these conversations? Do you feel drawn to join in any of them? What, if anything, do you feel you would like to say? Who would you like to have a 'one-to-one' with? Feel free, in your imagination, to go up to that person and express whatever it is that you would like to say or ask. Do you feel drawn to speak to Jesus in a personal way? Let this conversation take its course. Speak to him of whatever is in your heart, and listen to his response. Notice the look on his face (if you can) and the tone of his voice. In a significant meeting with a friend, you would be very observant of the 'body language' and the unspoken feelings passing between you. Do the same now with Jesus, if you feel drawn to do so.

You might like to let your imagination roam over one or both of the central events of the scene. Mary comes in to the room carrying a container of precious ointment, to pour over Jesus' feet. Imagine her feelings as she does so. How do *you* feel? (For example, some people may feel drawn to make their own offering of what is most precious to them; others may feel aloof and distant from the action, or embarrassed or disturbed. Don't *judge* your reaction – simply notice it.) Judas objects to what he regards as a waste. Listen to his reaction and notice how you feel. Do either of these two incidents pick up any memories in you, reminding you of anything in your own life? Just notice which, if either, draws you in to it. Notice your own role in all of this: maybe as an observer, not involved, or perhaps you find yourself identifying with Mary, Martha, Lazarus, Judas, one of the disciples, or Jesus himself. *Anything* can happen in imagination: don't put up any resistance to whatever floats up into your 'scene', even if you feel that it isn't the 'right' way to respond. There is no right and wrong way in prayer. Whatever is happening in your prayer has something to show you about your relationship with God and his movement in your heart.

After prayer – reflection

This kind of prayer, if you find that you are comfortable with it, can help you to discover a great deal about what is happening between you and God in the depths of your heart. But this will only be helpful if, after a period of prayer, you spend a few minutes *reflecting* on how it was and what seemed to be happening. (See Chapter 4.)

Let's suppose, for example, that you felt quite remote from Mary and her act of anointing, but Judas' words made you 'sit up and take notice'. What caused that change in your level of attention? Anger with Judas, perhaps, or impatience with Mary, or what? Notice your findings and ponder what they may be showing you – about yourself, or about your circumstances or situation, about any 'agenda' that is important to you right now?

Look back, in your reflection, especially over any 'conversations' you had in your prayer. Just as you might review a conversation with someone that happened at work, or in the family, taking in what was said, how it was said, what the implications were, etc., so too you will find it helpful and revealing to look back at any prayer conversations, especially if you were able, in your prayer, to speak to Jesus.

Two books that may help you further in you explorations of imaginative prayer are:

Six New Gospels by Margaret Hebblethwaite (Geoffrey Chapman, 1994)
Imagine That! by Marlene Halpin (Brown Roa, Iowa, USA, 1982)

17. BETWEEN FRIENDS

Prayer as conversation

If, in prayer, we are really seeking a personal relationship with God, then surely one way in which such a relationship would grow and be expressed would be in the course of *conversation*. This, after all, is the most obvious way of developing friendship in human relationships. Does the notion of holding a conversation with God make any sense in the life of prayer?

Then again, in our human friendships, our conversations are not limited to a single person. We hold conversations in different ways with different people, and, most importantly, our friendship with one particular person will very often lead us to meet, and enter into relationship with, others. We speak of a *circle of friends*. And we also frequently depict the Trinity as a circle of unbroken relationship between the Father, the Son and the Holy Spirit. Can prayer lead us into the mystery of this communion of friendship?

And can our conversations with God help us to understand more deeply the unbroken networks of communication that hold our human lives together? For example:

• The inner dialogue in which we are continually engaged, between God's creation and our own senses;
• The outer dialogues that we hold with each other, as we seek to understand ourselves and our hearts' desires.

And finally, the difficult, yet unavoidable question: how can we be sure that it is God 'speaking' to our hearts in prayer, and not just some script that we have written for ourselves?

Conversations with God

What might it mean to enter into a conversation with God? Isn't it a bit like trying to use a transistor radio to tune into the meaning of the universe? Isn't a conversation with God just a rather inflated way of describing what is really a conversation with ourselves?

In a way it is, I think. Yet in a way not so. We enter, in prayer, into 'conversations' which are in one sense only a dialogue between our own conscious *and unconscious* self. Yet we also believe – and I think we know, from heart-experience – that there is something – Someone – much greater than our mere selves at the heart of ourselves. We believe that our innermost centre is mysteriously and eternally connected to the heart of all that is, whom we call God. We believe, when we pray, that it is the Holy Spirit who prays in us, and that he indeed fulfils his promise to draw this hidden centre of ourselves into the heart of God. Prayer rests on this trust.

Do such conversations have any real value, or are they just a pious pastime? May I just share a small snippet of one such conversation with you, and invite you to judge for yourself what might be going on when we talk to God about what is on our minds? In this example, I had been meditating on the Fall, and on the judgement on Adam to 'till the soil from which God had created him'. It had seemed like a sentence to a long term in a labour camp, doing work that appeared to have no results:

'Prayer takes me back to Eden this morning in my imagination. I stand still for a moment, in your presence, preparing to enter into prayer, and I feel myself standing in the courtroom, all my untruth exposed to you, and waiting for your verdict. I feel the chill of apprehension in the room around me.

You begin to speak. You tell me that I must till the ground from which you took me, just as you did yourself.

> **Jesus**: 'I tilled the ground where I found myself – the ground out of which the Father created my earthly being.'
> **M.**: 'It sometimes seems so pointless, Lord. Like loosening the knot on a gate, for people to pass through, when you know very well that someone will come along and tie it up again.'
> **Jesus**: 'It often seemed pointless to me too. My family and neighbours would never take me seriously and I often doubted even myself. And *was* it pointless?'
> **M.**: 'What can I say? Here we are, 2000 years later, knowing that we *know* you. But even now, knowing your risen life, we seem to make so little impact anywhere. A small group of people gather, listen, pray, grow, and then disperse. Or we look further out and see the raging

darkness around us, enveloping even those we love ....'

Jesus:'... a small group gather, listen, pray, grow, and then disperse ... exactly the pattern of my own life .... So why do you keep on tilling?'

M:'It's the only way I can stay true to myself.'

Jesus:'And so it was for me.'

M:'Tilling means staying precisely there, with the soil from which you took me ....'

Jesus:'And tilling means coaxing, not bullying. Gently urging the earth into freedom and fruitfulness. Your tilling is to be done with a small garden fork, not with a JCB.'

M.:'And if the squirrels keep digging up my bulbs?'

Jesus:'Keep planting more. And pray for the squirrels.'

And I see, this morning, that your commandment to till the ground is not a punishment, but a call to share in your work of redemption and healing and life-restoring.'

Notice in this snippet how the imagined words of Jesus work as a wise soul-friend might: they reflect back to me what is really coming from my heart and from my deep desire. They bring me up against challenging questions about what I really want. And they point me to parallels in Jesus' own life that are obvious once they are pointed out, and which encourage and strengthen me. Though, psychologically speaking, they are, of course, coming from my own psyche, spiritually they are also coming from the Holy Spirit, working in me through my own mental and psychological processes, my own experience and memories and emotions, to show up the dark and light patches in me and lead me forwards towards a new bit of growing. You could even compare such a conversation (and indeed all forms of personal prayer) with an x-ray exposure. It shows up parts of myself that cannot readily be seen in everyday consciousness.

So don't be afraid to engage in conversation with the Lord (also called, more formally, a *colloquy*). You can pour out whatever you are feeling, and know that he will receive it in love and compassion. You can express your anger with him. He is more than big enough to take it! But listen to his side of the dialogue too. It might surprise you! And sometimes this element of startling and joyous surprise can be a true hallmark of the authenticity of your prayer. You may find yourself exclaiming, from time to time:'I can't think where *that* came from; that was the last thing I would have said myself.' Let such surprises both delight, and enlighten you. They come from depths of yourself that only God has fathomed, and they are true gift.

Meeting new friends

It would be a strange kind of friendship that never introduced the friend to other friends and family. Going home to meet the relatives can be daunting in human life, but it is a vitally necessary part of the growth of a friendship. We all know that friendship rarely survives in isolation. As I write we have a young Hungarian guest staying with us for a couple of weeks, to learn the language and see something of our country. When asked what she would especially like to do, she responded, among other things, that she would like to meet our daughter's friends. And what could be more natural than to introduce a new friend to our old friends?

Yet still it came as a strange idea to me at first that God might want to introduce me to some of his other friends too! And the difference with God, of course, is that his friends may be found anywhere, among the living and the dead, the saints and the sinners, the past and the present. We are in for some surprises when God takes us 'to meet the family'!

What can happen, when he does, can become a kind of three-dimensional conversation, or, as it is called more formally in some traditions 'a triple colloquy'. Such a conversation often begins with some human member of the communion of saints (Mary, for example), who then leads us to Jesus, who in turn takes us to the Father. This is a very valuable way of deepening prayer and allowing it to lead us gently from our own human history into God's deepest mystery.

An example may help to illustrate the dynamic of such a conversation:

> I woke up just after 5 a.m. and felt as if the night was over. Something seemed to call me to you, and to prayer. The house was silent. I trod softly, trying to avoid the squeaky floorboard on the landing. I lit the candle. All I could say was: 'You called me, Lord; here I am.'
>
> You drew me closer, into the circle of candlelight, simply accepting me into your own warmth and holding me gently in your magnetic heart.
>
> I brought myself to stillness – it didn't seem so difficult in this

borderland between sleep and consciousness. The darkness and the silence held no distractions. The distractions and obstructions were all within myself. I could see this much more clearly in the darkness. Strange, how the darkness can clarify our vision . . . .

I let my prayer take the form of a Triple Colloquy. I searched for Mary. I found her in her own little house in the village. It wasn't so difficult to knock on her door – like seeking out a friend – an older, wiser friend – who I knew, with heart-knowledge, could lead me to you. She was a soul-friend, and I had no fear in approaching her. She welcomed me, and drew me into her home. We talked for a while. Then she invited my to visit her garden.

The garden was an open space right in the centre of her house. A kind of open court-yard, circular, and alive with water, leaping up in fountains or flowing down waterfalls. The water was so clear and alive. I knew that it was the living water, and that she was answering my prayer to lead me to you.

Some of the fountains were leaping high and strong. I thought of some of the people I know in whom the living water rises in a surge. Others were only just alive, and some were totally stopped. And the waterfalls – they seemed like a flow of grace coming down from all those who have gone before us.

'If you are looking for my Son,' she said, 'he is over there.' At first I couldn't see anyone – the sight of those fountains was so over-whelming. Then I saw the figure of a man kneeling on the ground beside one of the fountains. It was one of the weaker ones, and he was gently unclogging it with his fingers. His whole attention was focused on the clogged-up fountain. I knew that it was you. I watched your face as you worked. There was no reproach, no blame, no anger. Only tenderness, and an overriding desire to free the fountain into life again.

Mary led me to you. I knelt down beside you. You welcomed me silently, not interrupting your work, yet holding me, too, in the full-ness of your loving attention. I knew that what you were doing for that little fountain you were also doing for me and my clogged-up heart. I begged you to do it, even if it meant using a steel brush on me sometimes (and it has!) because the desire of my inner fountain to flow free was so much more powerful than anything else.

'Let me take you to the Father', you said, turning your gaze towards me. I wondered, apprehensively, where and how 'the Father' might be, and whether he would accept me. Then you took my hand, drew me into your arms, and together we seemed to sink down into the infinite source of the water that was feeding all the fountains. I recognised the place! That was the amazing thing. I knew where I was, because I had been there before, at a well-remembered time when I had felt especially close to you and in deep consolation. I was with you in that warm pool of love that had enveloped me so un-expectedly at that time. My deepest desire had found its source. When you took me to the Father, *I knew where I was!*

In these graced moments of prayer I sensed something of the Father's great desire to express himself in our lives, and I felt some-thing of the power of his Spirit that translates that desire into a lived reality – the only Reality that there is.

Yet even as I touched the heart of the mystery, my own heart was darkened again by the knowledge of the untruth and the sin that clogs the outflow of that divine self-expression. My heart darkened and the vision faded. Yet the vision is not lost, because you are there again, kneeling beside the failing springs, searching out, with gentle fingers, the source of the obstruction. Search me, Lord, and know me, and free me from my sin, I beg you. Free me from the lesser attach-ments that block the outflow of your life in me.

Again, you turn towards me, your face alight with love, and joy that my desire is meeting yours. You take my hands again. 'The hands of my friends will do this work as well', you tell me. 'They will tend the failing springs in others, gently nurturing the renewal of their flow. This is how to set the captives free, and to unbind what is bound. This is the whole desire of the Father, to express his love in every human life, and this is our task, the task of us all together, to dissolve every-thing that obstructs that flow, by touching it with love.'

Listening to our senses

Conversations in human life depend heavily, as we all know, on body language. So much of what we communicate to each other is not expressed in words at all, but in our unconscious gestures, movements, tones of voice or other physical signals. We speak to each other constantly by means of body language, and we 'receive' these signals from each other through the medium of our five senses.

Such dialogue, being independent of words, can exist between people who have no knowledge of each others' language. It can even exist between human beings and animals, as anyone who owns a pet will testify. So it might well be a useful channel by which God will communicate with us, through his creation, as perceived through our senses.

You might like to listen in to this 'prayer conversation' with the three persons of the Trinity:

> **Father**: 'I created your eyes, that you might see all that I have created.'
> **Son**: 'I opened your eyes, so that you might see the hidden mystery of things.'
> **Holy Spirit**: 'I am the Light, that reveals all this to you.'
> **Father**: 'I created your ears, that you might hear the sound of my creation: its songs and its cries, its power and its subtlety.'
> **Son**: 'I opened your ears, so that you might respond to the crying and the laughter of creation.'
> **Holy Spirit**: 'I am the empty space, where sound resounds.'
> **Father**: 'I created your taste-buds, so that you might taste my creation in all its flavours.'
> **Son**: 'I opened up your taste-buds to respond to sweet and bitter, fresh and stale.'
> **Holy Spirit**: 'I am the discernment who guides you to choose what is wholesome and leave aside what is harmful to you.'
> **Father**: 'I created your nose, so that you might receive all the signals of scent that my creation produces.'
> **Son**: 'I opened up your sense of smell, so that you might respond to the scents of life and turn from those of death.'
> **Holy Spirit:** 'I am the attraction who draws you to the scents of growth and life, of flowers, fruit and fresh summer mornings, of salt-spray and new-mown hay and baking bread and rising yeast. I am the warning who repels you from the stench of death and staleness and rot and waste and all that corrodes and pollutes.'
> **Father**: 'I created your nerves, your skin, your fingertips, so that you might have feeling for my creation.'

Son: 'I opened up your sense of touch, and turned it into sensitivity, knowing both pain and pleasure, wounding and delight.'

Holy Spirit: 'I am the tenderness, that exposes your heart to the overflow of love and the stabs of pain. For tenderness carries both, knows both, unites both into the mystery of life and growth.'

Three persons, and five senses, and finally, the encircling silence with which prayer begins and ends. See the silence, hear the silence, taste and smell and feel the silence, that is Nothing, containing Everything. The great creating Circle in which All IS.

Healing encounters

A rather special form of 'conversation with God' can take the form of a three-way conversation in your imagination between yourself, Jesus and another person who has hurt you or is for some reason estranged from you. Sometimes this kind of scenario can make it possible for you, with the Lord alongside, to face feelings that you would not be able to express in a real conversation with the person concerned.

Just let yourself be in a place, in your imagination, where you feel safe, and invite the Lord to be there with you, maybe telling him about the problem you have with this person. Then, when you feel ready, draw the person, in your imagination, into the safe place with you, and express, through Jesus, what you are really feeling. Then give the other person an opportunity to say how he or she is feeling about things. Finally, you might turn to Jesus and ask him to share his truth and his love with you both. Just notice what suggests itself to you during this period of prayer. It may shed real light on the difficulties and offer you a breakthrough in the deadlock.

God speaking?

The big question: 'How do I know that this is God speaking to my heart and not my own mental script' cannot be side-stepped. It goes far beyond the questions arising in 'conversational prayer'. It can equally be asked of all that we call 'revelations' or 'insights' or 'enlightenments' in prayer. Are they from God, or merely from ourselves?

The same considerations apply as those we looked at in Chapter 16 in the context of imaginative meditation. In short:

• What comes from God will stay with us, take root, deepen and grow, and eventually bear fruit in our lives. What comes only from ourselves and the mental scripts we can write will not have a very long shelf life before it fades into oblivion.

• What comes from God will tend to turn our attention *away* from ourselves and towards God, his people, and his creation. What comes merely from ourselves will often be found to be centred on ourselves and the furtherance of our own personal kingdoms.

You will know a conversation by its fruits, but you will need to give those fruits time to ripen. One way of encouraging this ripening process is to practise 'deepening in' on what seems to be most significant in our prayer, in the ways suggested in Chapter 12.

Spiritual conversations

And there are other conversations which, as Christians, we are urged to engage in. These are serious conversations with each other, and with other people, about our relationship with God.

We all know that we are called to 'spread the Gospel', and we may have widely differing views on how we can best do this in our own circumstances. This is not a book about mission and evangelisation in this particular sense, but there are two ways of entering into 'spiritual conversations' with others that have a place in these reflections on ways of meeting God in personal prayer:

We can share our inner journey by talking with a 'soul-friend', in the ways suggested in Chapter 23. This is an invaluable way of deepening our relationship with God in the companionship of another believer who will listen to our story and help us discern God's action in it.

We can listen ourselves, with the same non-judgemental love, to the stories of other people, without any attempt to 'convert' or correct them. This provides fertile soil in which the seed of their faith can take root and grow, and it is perhaps among the most precious gifts that one human being can give to another.

A shared time of mutual discovery, silently companioned by God.

TAKING IT FURTHER ...

If the idea of 'talking to God' is new to you, try sitting down in your prayer space, maybe even with a cup of tea of coffee, and talking over the issues that concern you, just as you would with a friend. When you do this, take off your 'Sunday suit' and just be who you really are. Tell him exactly how you feel about things, including your anger and frustration.

Take an opportunity to engage in an in-depth conversation with a friend, or even with a person you may not know very well. As far as you both feel comfortable, try exploring something of what you are both about. This is as much an exercise in listening as in talking. A conversation of this kind is not an exercise in 'outreach' or evangelisation, but a shared time of mutual discovery of what is most important to you both.

A friend, who had never heard of the 'triple colloquy' and would probably not have felt drawn to practise it if she had, was meditating one day with a rather striking and unusual picture showing (a modern) Mary sitting at the sea-shore, holding her child in her arms. The Child Jesus is at once both allowing himself to be held in her embrace, but also straining towards something beyond it. He is reaching out his hand and pointing to a bright star in the sky above them.

The picture she was using is a 'triple colloquy' in itself. The viewer's gaze is first drawn to Mary's face, which is full of love and trust, yet also touched by sorrowful apprehension. She is gazing at her little Son, and our eyes are led by hers to him. She, as it were, leads us, or introduces us to him. He, in turn, is pointing to the stars, and to all that is 'beyond', to all that suggests the invisible origin of creation in 'the Father'.

You might like to ponder my friend's personal response to this picture. Notice how she 'listens in', first to Mary's words to her Child, then to Mary's invitation to Jesus to talk to the Father about what he is seeing and feeling, and finally, to the conversation Jesus tells her the Father has had with him and the peace-giving, trust-restoring effect it leaves in both their hearts.

Star of Wonder, Star of Joy
Not now, my love, not yet,
You can run free when you're older,
Stay with me and come to bed
For the night is growing colder.

Yes, I know you want a star,
A brilliant, sparkly shining light,
And one day you will, my love,
And you'll make the world so bright.
You'll hold it in your hand,
Yes, for all the world to see;
No, I don't know how it'll happen
But I know that it will be.
So be patient, dearest love,
And make the most of having fun,
For the day will come to pass
When you will know you are God's Son.

Pick your shells up now, my love,
We must go home right away,
Say goodnight to star of hope
Until your glory comes to stay.
We'll tell God all about it
When you're kneeling quiet to pray,
You can tell me what he says, dear,
If he talks to you today.

'He says he loves us mother,
Not to worry, just to wait.'
And she watched him fall asleep
And she pondered on his fate.
Such a joy was in her hands
Never failing to amaze
As she knelt beside his bed
Lost in wonder, love and praise.

(R. A. Hulme)

For help in approaching God in the intimacy of friendship, see *God and You* by William A. Barry SJ (Paulist Press, 1987).

18. BETWEEN A ROCK AND A HARD PLACE

Prayer when life is hurting

A pilgrim's first steps into the goldmine of personal prayer can feel like entering a realm of pure joy. The sense of being drawn ever more closely to God is truly an experience of 'consolation', which, in its original sense, means being 'with the sun', or in the presence of the very source and sustainer of our being.

Yet all of us know that the journey leads, inevitably, through valleys of shadow and darkness, where we can almost forget that we ever felt the warmth of the 'sun' in our hearts. But notice the word is *through* (not *to*) valleys of darkness, because God's presence in our lives *is* like the sun – it is always there, holding us in being with its never-failing energy, even when the clouds are down and we cannot see it, or even feel its effects. God is the eternal reality, *in whom we live and move and have our being*, and the things in our lives that block our awareness of that eternal reality are only temporary. They do not have the final word, just as the sun is permanently there, energising our physical lives, and the clouds, however depressing and long-lasting, are temporary. They can block the sun for a while, but they have no power to destroy it.

Even so, the cloud-times can very easily come to dominate our lived experience, and prayer that tries to skirt around the pain that pierces so much of our human living, can never be authentic. Where is God in those darknesses? Is there a place for prayer, or any point to prayer, when life is hurting?

The rock . . .

The prophet Elijah hit the rock, when he spoke out to King Ahab of God's anger and its consequences, and had to flee himself into the desert as a result. (1 Kings 17:2–6) Perhaps you might like to put yourself in Elijah's place for a few minutes, by becoming aware of any situation in your own life that feels like 'the rock'. Perhaps a situation in which there seems to be absolutely no way forward, or a relationship that causes you pain and shows no hope of any improvement, or a memory that holds you captive in resentment or fear. Let your personal circumstances show you your own 'desert', and spend a few minutes there with Elijah.

We find him in the middle of nowhere, in the Wadi Cherith, an exile and a frightened fugitive, full of doubts about his own mission, and about God's fidelity, and close to starvation. Two chapters later he is again on the run, this time close to suicidal despair, begging God to 'take my life'.

Now notice what happens, in each case. In the Wadi Cherith we are told two facts: the first is that Elijah 'drank from the stream'; secondly, 'the ravens brought him bread in the morning and meat in the evening'. Two chapters later, out in the wilderness near Beersheba, we are told that the despairing prophet falls into an exhausted sleep, 'but an angel touched him' and urged him to eat, to nourish himself. When he looked around, he found 'a scone baked on hot stones, and a jar of water', and 'he ate and drank'.

I find these stories among the most encouraging in all the Scriptures, perhaps because, like all of you surely, I know how it feels, in my own small way, to feel like Elijah on this 'hard rock'. And there is something that rings true in my memory about that stream, about the food brought, apparently out of the blue, by the ravens, about the angel's touch and the unexpected meal, along with the gentle persuasion to 'take and eat'.

I think that these pictures of Elijah's agony can bring us closer to an understanding of God's invisible presence in our own 'hard rock' experiences in life. We can turn this story into something real and alive for ourselves if we can get in touch with the ways in which God does, or ever has done, something similar for us, or for those we love. Try reflecting, for example on:

• Times when you have been 'down and out' and some little signal of encouragement came to you, perhaps from a totally unexpected source.
• Areas of your life that feel like deserts, with nothing to cheer or encourage you, but where, if you look back and look hard, you can see a tiny trickle of water that has somehow kept you going against the odds. What was, or is, that life-saving stream for you?

- Days, or months, or years of despair that have been punctuated now and again by an 'angel's touch' that restored your faith in yourself and in humanity. Who touched you then? Can you be the bringer of an 'angel's touch' to someone else who is at the end of the line?
- Times when, perhaps, you have wound yourself down into exhaustion and maybe cried yourself to sleep, then woken up to find a renewed calm, a fresh perspective, new sustenance for tomorrow's journey. Not a banquet! Just a day's supply of baked scones and clear water. Just enough for one more step into the future. And a loving word that urges you to 'choose life' by taking and eating. Who brought you that midnight feast, and how did you react? Now, with hindsight, can you see God's hand in it?

All these little signs and wonders are the proof that the sun does not cease to shine even when the clouds block our view of it. Prayer can help us to take hold of these God-given life-savers, and let his strength carry us one step further through the darkness. It can also suggest ways in which we might work with him in feeding others who have come to the end of their resources.

Prayer, if it is honest, does not deny the darkness in our hearts and the anguish in our lives, but it can lead us to the streams in our desert and the morsels of food that we never expected. A very effective way to discover this water and bread, or to become aware of the 'angel's touch' is to stay faithful especially to those few minutes each day when we look back over the past twenty-four hours of our life and notice where God has been present to us. This can be the place in which we are enabled to do what Elijah did next:

> *'He got up and ate and drank, and strengthened by that food he walked for forty days and forty nights until he reached the mountain of God.'*
>
> *(1 Kings 19:8).*

. . . And the hard place

The hardest place of all, in our human experience, is the Calvary place, the Gethsemane garden, where Jesus plumbed the depths of all human grief and despair. Can we ever connect to this kind of pain, and if so, can it help us to understand and grow through our own?

We have looked, in Chapter 16, at the possibility of praying the Gospel stories imaginatively. This kind of prayer can (and certainly eventually *will*) lead us into an imaginative sharing of Jesus' last days on earth. And there it can reveal to us the very personal ways in which we play our own part in the events of those days. When we enter the scenes of Holy Week in our imagination, we are inviting the Lord to take us into the very heart of the matter. There, if we will let him, he will open up to us those ways in which our personal pain and grief connects to his, and the way in which he, in his agony, is connecting to us personally, in ours.

Some people find, for example, that they are standing alongside Pilate, washing their hands of responsibility in particular dilemmas of daily life that call for decisive commitment. Others, who maybe complain loudly about violence on our TV screens or in our streets, discover to their shame that they are playing a part themselves in the violence against Jesus. Some sense within themselves the instinct to run, or to deny any knowledge of this hunted criminal who was once their friend. Then again, some people discover a powerful longing in their hearts, to be present to the Lord in his hours of agony, to follow him, to offer him the drink he asks for or to tend his broken body. There are endless possibilities, and as always in this kind of prayer, you will not be able to predict where you may find yourself. From one day to another, your place in these events will change. And all the while you will be discovering things about yourself that you had perhaps not yet been aware of.

In all of this, always keep in mind the golden rule:

Do not judge yourself, or others. God will lead you himself to where he wants you to be, and he will do that leading with tenderness and with infinite love.

Most surely there will be aspects of yourself that will cause you to grieve for your own part in the world's Calvary, and just as surely there will be aspects of yourself that will reveal your own deep longing to be close to the Lord. Just let your prayer bring up for you those *particular* ways in which *your* experience of life, with its pain and its shame, as well as its faithfulness and trust, connects to the experience of Jesus in his suffering and death.

Living your own hurts in the Gospel light of Jesus' suffering has some important consequences:

• It shifts your focus, away from the immediate pain in your own life, towards the even greater pain in *his*, and in his world's. This is the first movement towards healing, and the healing that he is offering to you is not just for you but, in some mysterious way, for the entire human family. When your pain is joined with his, it becomes part of his redeeming love.

- It will lead you through Friday to Sunday, because, as we noticed earlier, the sun, and not the clouds are the permanent reality – God's indestructible life, running through our own human living, and not the terrible, but temporary darkness of our sin and brokenness.

How often have you heard the question asked, or even asked it yourself, in the face of some terrible disaster, or some painful immovable blockage in your own life: 'Where is God in this suffering?'

If you have the courage to enter into the suffering, death and resurrection of the Lord in your personal prayer, you may find his question answering your own: 'Where are *you* in mine?' If you let him, he will gently show you where you are in his, and this will become a way in which he can open up your heart and your life to his healing.

Ground between the stones

I have called this chapter 'Between a rock and a hard place', because something very creative can happen when we find ourselves crushed between two overwhelming forces.

Just as wheat is ground between the millstones, and turned into flour, so it sometimes can feel that we are being ground down into dust by the opposing forces and conflicting demands of our lives. While the grinding is going on we can feel only the pain of it and we lose all sense of any purpose or greater good that might come of it.

But just try looking back over some of the really painful times of your life. Can you, with hindsight, see any good thing that came to be as a result of those hard times? Perhaps it is something intangible ... you may have gained a new insight into other people's needs or fears, or a greater patience with their weaknesses. You may even have discovered, through the very things that you lack and long for, that there is something *beyond* life's surface wants and wishes, and your very emptiness may have been a pathway to a deepening closeness with God.

Something creative can happen
when we are crushed between
two overwhelming forces.

Every child comes to birth through the real agony of labour through
which the mother must live, and St Paul speaks of all creation being in one
huge process of giving birth. A great deal of human suffering is unnecessary and destructive, and can and should be resisted and alleviated. Yet it
remains true that each individual's personal experience of pain can sometimes be labour pain – the pain that is grinding wheat to be turned into
flour, and baked into bread for ourselves and for others.

One of the fruits of prayer and reflection, as we have been exploring it, is to help us to distinguish between the chaff and the wheat in both our negative and our positive experiences. On the positive side, the 'chaff' is the mere pleasure that may give us a temporary boost, but will never satisfy the deepest desires of our hearts, while the 'wheat' is the joy that can never be shaken, whatever life throws at us. When it comes to our life's hurting, the 'chaff' is the pain that we are called to resist and reject, because it is diminishing us, or others, as human beings. The 'wheat' is the labour pain that is drawing us beyond ourselves, to a wholeness in God and in each other, just as it drew Jesus through Calvary into the light of the resurrection.

TAKING IT FURTHER ...

You might like to invite your memory and your experience to be your teachers in the art of discerning between the wheat and the chaff. If you look back to past times, just notice which kinds of painful experience have, in the end, led to growth of some kind in your life, and which have only left you feeling broken. This kind of reflection will help you to recognise and value the 'wheat', and to co-operate increasingly with God's work in your heart, as he grinds the harvest of your experience between the rock and the hard place, in order to bake living bread for his hungry children.

When, in the past, have you 'hit the rock'? Remember that time in prayer. As you look back, can you see what morsels of food and trickles of water kept you going through that time? They might have been the words or actions of a friend, or a stranger, or some incident or encounter that changed your perspective in some way. Express your thanks to God for this healing touch in whatever way feels right for you.

Choose one of the Gospel narratives of Jesus' last days on earth, and read it through several times, prayerfully and peacefully. Notice your reactions. With what parts or with which people of the narrative do you find that your feelings are most powerfully engaged? What do your feelings reveal about the pain in your own life and how it connects to the suffering of Jesus? Now let your prayer move forward, when you are ready, from the agony of Friday, through the dark emptiness of Saturday, to the dawn of Sunday morning. Where has the resurrection light shone in your life?

19. GOING ROUND IN CIRCLES?

Contemplation in action

How much stillness was there in *your* day today? And before you start to feel guilty, just stop to remember what has been going on. The demands have been coming in from all quarters, many of them conflicting. Children, colleagues, partners, relatives, friends, neighbours – some combination of these will have been clamouring for your time and your attention in some way. The phone will have rung, perhaps many times, or letters and bills will have arrived on your doormat, asking for replies or payment or some kind of action. And alongside all of that you will have been trying to do your normal day-to-day tasks – cleaning, shopping, thinking what to give the family to eat, attending to birthday presents, organising parties, keeping the home going, keeping the car running, keeping the garden in order, to say nothing of holding your own in a paid job, or struggling through the pain and bureaucracy of being unemployed. For many people today life seems to be just one long relentless round of keeping things going and unravelling life's knots. Small wonder that you feel as if you are perpetually running round in circles. Small wonder that there is no time for *you* in your day, and even less time for God.

But I hope you have discovered, in the journey we have shared so far, that God *has* been present in this endless round in ways you may not previously have recognised, and that little corners of peace *can* be carved out of this rat-race that seems to dominate so much of our lives. Nevertheless, coming to some kind of stillness remains one of the greatest obstacles to prayer for many people. In this chapter we might pause to notice that, while the still centre is an essential anchor-point for prayer, the busy-ness all around the edges also has its part to play in our journey to God and to wholeness.

Finding the anchor point

Coming to quietness *externally* is no big problem for most of us. We usually find it quite easy to still ourselves physically – perhaps because we were constantly reminded as children to 'sit still' and 'stop fidgeting'. But maybe that was one of the reasons why we turned our activity *inwards*. Lively, exuberant children, forced to sit still, find an outlet for their suppressed energy in the racing thoughts of their growing minds. Why should we hope to be any different? So we face a much greater difficulty when we try to still our *thoughts and minds* into a receptive peacefulness. And if we do manage to come to equilibrium in our minds, to allow space for prayer, we still have to overcome the hurdle of our turbulent *feelings* and the stirrings of our restless hearts.

How often do we come to the end of a day and sink, exhausted, into bed with words like 'I haven't stood still all day' or 'My feet haven't touched the ground today'? Or has anyone said something like 'I'll catch you later' to you today? As if we are spending our whole lives running a race and even our friends have to sprint to 'catch up with us'! Sinking those 'ten feet down', when everything around us is spinning us in a relentless perpetual motion is a bit like dropping anchor in a stormy sea.

The time has come, perhaps, to reflect on how prayer can make it possible to be connected to a 'still centre' of ourselves, an anchor point, even while everything seems to be spinning around us. A brief excursion into an imaginative prayer picture might help to clarify things. See if it speaks to you in any way . . ..

The cartwheel in the forest

One day in prayer I let myself imagine what 'freedom' might be like. In my imagination, I found myself becoming a piece of wood lying on the floor of a beautiful forest. For a while I just stayed there, enjoying the view, thinking to myself, how wonderful it felt to be free, to be myself in this lovely forest, with no interference from anyone and no tasks or duties or difficult relationships to worry about.

Then my dream of liberty was cut short. Still in my imaginative prayer, I was picked up by a pair of strong, weathered hands, and examined. I felt exposed and helpless in the process. But worse was to follow. Those same strong hands took me and shaped me, planed and chiselled me into a totally new shape. I felt sore and resentful, and frightened at where this unfamiliar process might be taking me.

At last the painful work was finished, and the strong hands fitted me, gently, but very firmly, into a wheel. One end of me was fixed to the hub, the other end to the rim. I was just a spoke in this wheel, and I didn't particularly like my neighbouring spokes! What had become of my cherished freedom? As so often happens in prayer, the answer seemed to be a deafening silence! But nevertheless the prayer did yield its answer to my unspoken question . . ..

Gradually, but surely, the wheel began to *move*, and a voice somewhere inside me said: 'Do you want the freedom to stay where you are, in splendid isolation on the forest floor, or do you want the freedom to move on, in the community of all my people?'

The cartwheel gathered momentum. At one end of my being I experienced the dizzy feeling of spinning through time, space and circumstances that I could neither avoid, nor significantly influence. At my 'outer edge' – the layer of my consciousness – I spend most of my waking moments in this spinning state. But there is another 'end' of me, which is just as surely fixed to a still centre. Prayer takes me to that still centre. It connects all the holding, guiding, stabilising power of that central hub of my being to the spinning outer edges of my life. It holds me in real communion, whatever happens on the journey, however dizzily the wheel of my life may spin. It is the heart *and* the means of my own journey and the journey of all the human family.

And the cartwheel is a helpful picture of what it means to be 'the people of God'. On the surface of life we are all very different, often far apart, both in where we live and what we do and how we see things. But at the centre, in Christ, we are *one*. The closer we move towards that centre, the more clearly we are focused on it, the closer we will move towards each other. Even those who appear to be on opposite edges of the wheel's rim will draw closer to each other as they draw closer to Christ.

But the purpose of the wheel is to *move*. And it's worth reflecting on how that movement happens. *Not* through the efforts going on on the rim, however important they may feel to us. Not even through the prayer that is offered at the hub. But solely and simply by means of the drive shaft who is Christ, and who relies not on the power of our rims or the depth of our centred prayer, but on the empty space in our hearts where we acknowledge that neither action nor contemplation is ours to *achieve*, but his to *give*. That is the emptiness that makes space for God's driving energy that carries us and all his creation towards the Kingdom.

The turning wheel of our everyday
translates contemplation
into action.

The potter's wheel

I live in the Potteries, where many people know at first hand what the potter's craft is all about. And even the rest of us, who, like me, would never manage to raise a pot from that lump of clay spinning on the table, can find a helpful picture of prayer, and of our life and journey with God, in the picture of the potter's wheel.

In prayer we look for that kind of still and silent surrender that we could compare to the wet clay's yielding to the potter's touch. We are God's creatures. He creates us – we don't create ourselves. And when we do try to mould the world to our liking and shape our circumstances in the way we would like them to be, we very often get things badly wrong. To pray is to place ourselves in God's hands and trust that he, the Potter, will form us into the person he has dreamed we shall become – that unique part of his creation that will reveal our own personal something of who God is, when his Kingdom reigns.

But the pot needs more than just the clay, for its formation, and more than the Potter's skill alone. It *needs* the spinning wheel! Just as for my cartwheel in the forest, there has to be *motion*. The spinning of my life's hours and days, that sometimes seems so senseless and frenzied to me, may be precisely that spinning that is moving me, and all creation, forwards towards our destination in God. So often we would like nothing better than simply to 'stop the world and get off', but prayer does not allow us that kind of escape route from our lived reality. God is weaving his dream for us, and for all creation, not only in the stillness of our hearts, but in the whirling activity of our lived circumstances.

Of course, the spinning on its own doesn't get me anywhere unless it is all centred on that hub that we call God. We need the still centre *and* the spinning rim of ourselves, and the two together remind us that we are not just individual people seeking God and our own salvation, but we are all members of a community – the people of God, the Body of Christ. Prayer, to go deep, must become personal. But it must never become privatised!

Contemplation in action

The cartwheel and the potter's wheel can help us to understand where our prayer is *anchored*, and where it is *active*.

It is anchored in the *stillness of heart*, that we practise whenever we try to calm ourselves into a period of deliberate prayer. In this stillness we sink down below the surface storms and pre-occupations of our conscious lives and open ourselves to God in hope-filled expectation, simply listening to whatever the Holy Spirit may bring to our inner eyes and ears.

It becomes *active* when we begin to live out, in our daily lives, what we have learned in the deep quiet of prayer. It becomes active by changing the ways we see things and react to our circumstances, and by helping us to make decisions in the light of Gospel values. But it also becomes active, in ways that lie far beyond our understanding or imagination, by forming us (like potter's clay) into people who *make a difference* to the communities we live in – to our homes and workplaces, our neighbourhoods and parishes. The prayer of *each* of us affects *all* of us. The spoke goes nowhere until it becomes part of the wheel. And the wheel will not move freely if even one single spoke is missing or broken.

Encounter at the oasis

A Gospel woman who discovered both her anchor point and her call to action in a brief encounter with Jesus is the Samaritan woman who met the Lord at the well as she was fetching her daily water supply (John 4:5–30). Perhaps it's a hot, dusty day in high summer. The land is parched and dry. Jesus and his friends are walking through the countryside of a foreign region. They are tired, and hungry, and very, very thirsty. They stop beside an ancient well, that has stood there for many generations. The people from the next village have to come out here every morning and every night to fetch the water they need.

Jesus sits down on the edge of the well, to rest. His friends set off to the village to buy some food for their lunch. For a few minutes he is alone there, watching his friends disappearing in a heat haze, off to the village. Perhaps he wipes the sweat from his forehead and looks up. A woman is approaching, with a water jar, to draw water from the well. It isn't the thing to do, to talk to a strange woman, especially in this foreign, hostile region. He knows that, but still he doesn't hesitate to draw her into conversation. Perhaps she draws closer, sits down for a rest herself, looks into the face of this unexpected stranger . . . . They enter into conversation. Jesus, she discovers, knows her better than she knows herself. Just as the ancient well has its foundations in the history of both their peoples, so Jesus takes her to the foundations of herself. They 'drop anchor' in the silent midday heat. In Jesus she has found the still centre of herself.

But the wheel is made to move, and when their conversation is completed her contemplation turns into action:

'The woman put down her water jar and hurried back to the town to tell the people ....'

And her own response to all she has experienced while 'at anchor' in Jesus becomes the catalyst for something of a mass movement:

'This brought people out of the town and they made their way towards him.'

We can almost see the wheels of contemplation moving into action! And we know that, for ourselves too, this movement in our hearts and minds and lives has its origin, its energy and its guiding power in the still place where we are anchored to the Lord in prayer.

And thinking back to the prayer of the 'hard place' that we looked at in the previous chapter, it always encourages me to reflect on the fact that if the Samaritan woman had had the benefit of a mains water supply in her home, she would never have met Jesus, because she would not have needed to go to the well. How often do our apparent hardships, and our needs, lead us beyond the horizon of experience to the dawn of new light and understanding?

TAKING IT FURTHER ...

Try reading the story of the Samaritan woman for yourself in John 4:5–30, using the imaginative approach suggested in Chapter 16. Notice where the scene seems to take you. Notice your own 'well', which is wherever you personally encounter the Lord. Let yourself be there in his presence, simply contemplating the relationship you share together. Stay for as long as you wish in that sacred place, beside the well which has foundations deep in the source of 'who you are'.

Then let Jesus send you back to your 'village', the place in the world where you are called to live out the consequences of your prayer. Where does this call seem to be drawing you?

At the well of your prayer you have drawn the living water? What are you going to do with that water now?

Next time that you feel you are running round in circles, let the harassment or the dizziness you are feeling act as a trigger in your mind which says: 'STOP!' Try to stand still, just for a few moments. Take a few deep breaths and just imagine:

- Standing with the soles of your feet squarely on the ground, with deep roots going down into the earth beneath you, or
- Plunging your bucket down into the cool waters of a well and drawing up a draught of clear water, or
- Dropping anchor in the middle of a gale, and letting your life's boat come to stillness and security.

These moments of recollection will pass, but you will have touched into the true source of your energy, and you will be empowered to *move on*, because:

- Your feet are made for walking
- The water is for carrying back to the village
- The boat is built to sail.

20. THE RIVER DEEPENS

From words into silence: approaching
contemplative prayer

Called into the depths of God

Back at the beginning of this journey into prayer we looked at ways of praying with our own life's story, and we used the image of the river as a way of noticing the flow of our life so far, with its joys and its difficulties. Today I would like to invite you to reflect on another river, which always helps me personally to draw closer to God in prayer. This is the river described by the prophet Ezekiel, in his vision of his own relationship with God. If you would like to read it, you can find it in Ezekiel 47:1–12.

It describes a spring of fresh water gurgling up under the doorway to the temple. You might imagine the temple to be your own life, or your own innermost being, your heart, where God dwells. And the spring bubbles up as an expression from deep within you of your desire to be in a loving relationship with God and to express this relationship in prayer.

But the search for prayer is by no means always straightforward. See what happens to Ezekiel. He comes out of the temple by the north gate and is led all around the building, anti-clockwise, until he gets to the east gate and discovers the stream of prayer. With hindsight, he could have had an easier journey! He could have at least walked clockwise and cut out three-quarters of the circular journey round the temple! But we can all be wise with hindsight.

However convoluted and long-winded the path, let's assume that we have arrived at that 'east gate', and found that trickle of a stream that is flowing there – flowing out in the direction of the Dawn. Only a trickle, but full of hope and desire. We might follow it as it flows out into the unknown country of the rest of our lives . . . .

Ezekiel notices how his stream is deepening. How do you feel about *yours*? In Ezekiel's picture if we wander five hundred yards downstream and 'test the waters', we find ourselves still only ankle-deep. Prayer is happening, perhaps, but it is only lapping round our ankles, so to speak, and not making much difference yet to the way we live. Another five hundred yards and we are already knee-deep. Prayer is perhaps beginning to challenge us and become a force to be reckoned with. And still another five hundred yards on, we find ourselves waist-high in the water. Living with prayer is demanding a great deal from us, but God is also showing us his increasing trust in us, and sharing more and more of himself with us – for, after all, *he is the stream* that is flowing through our hearts and bringing us to the fullness of life.

And finally, when we have come the last five hundred yards down-stream, the trickle of prayer that we barely noticed at the beginning of its journey, has become a river so wide and deep that we can no longer cross it. We can only surrender ourselves totally to its power and let it carry us onward in faith to the sea of perfect communion with God and all his children which is our heart's destination. Will we ever dare to take that kind of risk? But notice what happens at this point in the journey into prayer . . .. So far we have been measuring the river, and noticing how it deepens. In our prayer journey too we tend to do this – to gauge 'how well we are doing', or 'how far we have come', and the truth is that a loving relationship cannot be weighed and measured, nor can one person's unique love of God, and his for that person, ever be compared with any other. When the river becomes too deep for our paddling and our wading, *then the focus changes*.

From now on, in Ezekiel's picture, the focus is on the river, rather than on the person who is experiencing it. See what happens as a result. When our focus turns away from ourselves and our 'achievements', and towards the river itself, we see something rather different of what the river is actu-ally about. We notice the trees growing alongside it, their roots watered by its flow, their branches bearing fruit in every season to feed God's hungry people. We see the plants and medicinal herbs along the riverbank, watered by its flow in order to bring healing to a broken world. And we see fisher-men dangling their rods in its waters, and drawing good catches of the teeming fish, to nourish their families. The more the river widens and deepens, the more abundant is the life that it sustains, until the whole of creation is brought to fruitfulness and the dry desert places burst into blossom.

I believe that this is more than a poetic piece of prophecy for the coming of God's reign in his world. I believe it is truly a picture of what prayer can become for *every* pilgrim. I believe it because, again and again I have seen people's struggle to find the 'east gate' and discover that tiny trickle – the first springing up of a desire to pray. And I have seen their disbelief, their wonder, their joy, as their little trickle has deepened and widened. I have seen them challenged by their prayer and by the joys and the pain that a personal relationship with God brings with it. And I have seen them at the point when their focus has shifted from themselves, to the desert plains through which the river of grace is flowing, and they have realised that prayer *is* that flow of grace, and that they themselves have become part of it.

Called into transformation

A few weeks ago I spent a day on the west coast of Wales, visiting friends, and we went for a long walk along the beach and among the sand dunes. We had the precious gift of time that day. Nothing was rushing us. We could linger for as long as we wished, and really see and experience the life of the shoreline.

This oasis in the midst of life's 'busy-ness' also happened to come at a time when a close friend had just been tragically bereaved. Untimely death was very much on our minds. And large, unanswered questions about the apparently senseless extinguishing of a young woman's life. Perhaps you can imagine something of our thoughts and our mood as we walked along the shore.

And perhaps for us, as for the first disciples who met the risen Lord on the shores of Galilee (John 21:1–14), there was a stranger on the shore, waiting to greet us, to invite us to share a barbecue breakfast, and to point our hearts to the side of our lives where the net-breaking catch of fish would be found so unexpectedly. Now, as I look back and reflect on that walk with friends, I can certainly see ways in which God made his presence known to us that day. And I would like to share just one of the treasures from that walk with you, because for me it was a picture of, and an invitation into, the kind of prayer that is literally transforming . . . .

The first clue was flying and fluttering in and out of the carpet of flowers that blanketed the grassy dunes – pink sea thrift and golden vetches, delicate lemon and purple violets, and tiny blue germander speedwells. And everywhere among them a host of perfect black and crimson

In our silent, trustful waiting,
we are letting God be God.

butterflies. We walked on, treading carefully, and our daughter stopped, as she had so often done as a little girl, to gaze in wonder at the wealth of little black and green tufted caterpillars crawling in the grass. It was hard to imagine that these little creatures would also soon be flying with black and crimson wings. We all knew about the transformation that awaited them: we knew the biology of it, but we had no felt experience of the miracle.

We sat down among the dunes to enjoy our picnic lunch, and as we sat there noticing all that was going on around us, our gaze was suddenly captured by the sight of what looked like dried up seedpods or half-dead leaves clinging to some of the grass-stalks. I would probably have been content to leave it at that, had not my friend pointed out that these were actually the pupae of the tiny butterflies we had seen. When I realised what she was saying, I looked at the little yellow 'seed-pods' in a very different light. Inside that still and silent pod an amazing act of transformation was taking place. To see the miracle happening before my eyes was breathtaking.

I was so thrilled by this discovery, that I looked up the life cycle of butterflies again when I got back, and read that the evolving caterpillar, about to enter the next phase of its 'Becoming', starts by spinning a thread, from its own body, to attach itself firmly to the stalk of a plant, that will hold it throughout the pupa stage. It seems to me that we do something like this when we allow God to draw us into what is often called 'contemplative prayer'. All that we can do, in such prayer, is to cling on to God, by a thread of silk spun out of our own deepest longings, and to trust him to hold us. What happens then seems to me very like the experience of the chrysalis. Of course we can't imagine what it is like to be a chrysalis, but at least we can surmise that this is a completely *passive* state. The busy caterpillar, whose daily task was to find food and to grow, now allows itself to become a passive being that hangs, quite still and silent, apparently doing nothing, and looking like a lifeless seedpod . . . .

But, of course, seedpods are very far from lifeless! They may look dormant, but they actually contain all the plant's tomorrows, just as wondrously as the ovaries of an unborn female child contain all the eggs that may ever become new life in the adult woman. And perhaps contemplative prayer is rather like that. It looks, and feels like nothing. In the depths of contemplation there is no active imagination at work, no thinking, no feeling, no image, no petition or intercession. What there *is*, is that slender line of connection, linking us to the God who holds us. And there is God, nothing but God, or as they say where I come from, 'Nobbut God'.

Waiting for the butterfly

A lovely and familiar picture of contemplative prayer is the one often mentioned of the French peasant who used to go into his parish church every day, without fail, for a period of quiet, when he would simply sit at the back of the church and gaze into the air. The parish priest noticed this, and one day he asked the man about his daily visits to the church, and what he was actually doing. This was the answer:

> *'I just look at God. And he looks at me. And we are content.'*

It all seems like nothing at all – perhaps the same kind of 'nothingness' that was happening as Jesus hung dying on the cross, like a pupa hanging by a thread to a stalk. But the butterfly book gave me one more piece of vital information. The pupa skin, it said, has holes in it, so that the evolving chrysalis can get oxygen, because in fact a great deal of energy is being expended there inside the pupa skin. It is the *energy of transformation*. That inert, dormant creature, hanging passively on a stalk, is, even as we gaze, being transformed from a hairy, greedy caterpillar, into a beautiful, life-renewing butterfly.

If you didn't know about butterflies, there is no way that you could possibly guess what miracle is happening there in the silent darkness of the pupa. And the same is true of the passive silence of deep contemplative prayer. Only God knows about our 'butterflies'. *We* still live in the realm of the caterpillar, who thinks that life is about active survival. But in contemplative prayer we are drawn beyond our caterpillar, trusting that the 'nothingness' is leading to 'everything', trusting in the butterfly that is still far beyond our imagination.

Letting creation teach us how ...

Quite probably most of us, if we think of contemplative prayer at all, regard it as something quite beyond us, and really only practised by a few 'contemplative' monks and nuns, whose whole lives are devoted to prayer. Yet I have heard it said, by respected and experienced spiritual guides, that contemplation is often given to those you would least expect – to harassed mothers, and people who think they 'can't pray', to children, to the sick and dying, to people with no head learning about prayer or Scripture or theology. God sometimes seems to speak, heart to heart, in this mysterious way, to the untaught and unpractised. None of us should imagine that the ways of contemplative prayer are closed to us, because God is always infinitely larger than all our expectations.

But how do we begin?

I suggest that creation itself gives us a gateway. In every moment that we live, a silent, invisible miracle of exchange is constantly taking place. We breathe out the air that our bodies no longer need, which is mainly carbon dioxide, a waste product for us, but the very thing that the green leaves on the trees and plants need to produce their own vital energy. So they receive our carbon dioxide and, through the process of photosynthesis, produce not only their own life energy, but also oxygen – a waste product for them, but the very thing we need to live. Whenever I stop my 'busy-ness' for a few moments to look around me, I am amazed at this arrangement, and it makes me think of prayer.

So perhaps a good way to open our hearts up to the gift of contemplation is simply to become still, and, quite literally, to breathe *out* our 'waste' – all that clogs us and deadens us, and to breathe *in* God's renewing life, as we breathe in the fresh oxygen that the plants have made for us. This simple, deliberate breathing exercise can become something like what the French peasant was doing as he 'just looked at God and God just looked at him'. We are simply becoming present to the mysterious exchange of life between ourselves and God. Nothing more. Nothing less. And there is no reason why any period of quiet might not become prayer of this kind, each inbreathing a silent expression of our heart's thankfulness and longing, each outbreathing a surrender of its aching.

And there may be other creatures who can help you cross the threshold of contemplation. If there is a baby in the family, try simply holding her in your arms as she sleeps, and letting God hold both of you in his. Nothing more. No deep thoughts. No search for meanings. Just be there.

A cat (if you are not allergic to them!) can also be a great aid to prayer. My own cat loves to sleep round my neck. At first I found this disturbing, but when he has settled into a particular hollow (perhaps where he can feel my pulse), he will lie there, quite still, just purring deeply, until he falls asleep and the purring ceases. When he does this, I let myself find 'a hollow' close to 'God's pulse', and let my own prayer become just a sleepy purr, and then the silence of content. Or you might discover prayer on a park bench. The other day I was in Hyde Park, and I spent a few minutes listening to the deep-throated cooing of the pigeons. My heart wanted to join them, because, in their way, they were engaged in contemplative prayer, simply expressing, in this peaceful murmur, the song of their hearts.

In your own home, prayer awaits you in the opening of a flower, or the drying of a butterfly's wings, the rising of your bread dough, or the steady, imperceptible development of a child. Spend time in silence, aware of the wonder that is being unfolded in your cakes and your children, your houseplants or your garden. For this is the essence of contemplative prayer – simple awareness, allowing God to be God, without trying to put the limitations of shape or meaning around him.

Contemplation, like all prayer, is pure gift, and not anything that we can 'achieve'. It happens when prayer becomes, wholly and utterly, the flow of God's grace alone, transforming the land it flows through, like Ezekiel's stream. Or it happens when we lose consciousness of our own part in it, and become simply receptors and carriers of grace. It happens when we realise that our transformation depends on nothing but God's grace and love, and, like the chrysalis, let go of all activity to try to achieve our own redemption.

When we try to describe it, we fail, for it lies beyond the world of words. We can open our hearts to it, by the practice of awareness, but we cannot bring it about, any more than we can force a flower to open or an egg to hatch. And in our silent, trustful waiting, we are acknowledging that God is God, the source and the destination, the means and the end of all our prayer, whatever form it may take.

TAKING IT FURTHER . . .

No words can lead you into wordlessness, but you might like to spend some time just gazing at the picture opposite. It is the photograph of a small baby gazing for the first time in her new life at a fuchsia flower, hanging down over her pram, in a garden centre. She is seeing the very first fuchsia for the very first time, and her eyes are wide with wonder and delight. She is seeing creation with God's eyes. She is actually in deep and joyous contemplation. She is in prayer. And probably she will never again pray with such effortless intensity.

But there will be moments in her life when this first profound awareness of the mystery of things will return. Perhaps when she falls in love. When she holds her own child in her arms. When she is transported by some moment of joy so fleeting, yet so solid that she knows she is in touch with her own deepest reality. We all know such moments, and we have explored something of their meaning in the pages of this book.

Must we wait until they visit us, like passing butterflies, who may, or may not, see us hiding shyly in the undergrowth, longing for grace yet unable to grasp it? I remember once, at the start of a retreat, being invited by my guide to spend a few hours simply walking round, with my eyes open, until something in the world around me caught my attention, and then just to

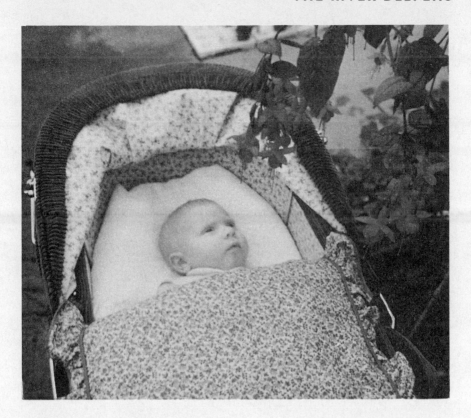

remain, quietly present to that presence. You might like to try this exercise for yourself, asking for the grace to see with God's eyes – or with Adam's eyes – to see some small part of creation as if for the very first time and with the very first human eyes, and then let your response pour out to God in silent wonder.

For a very helpful approach to contemplative prayer, see *Word into Silence* by John Main (Darton, Longman and Todd, 1980).

PART FOUR

STUMBLING BLOCKS AND STEPPING STONES

If only it were so easy . . .! I hope that I haven't left you wondering what-ever happened to all the very real reasons why prayer seems to fall apart so often. And I hope, too, that you may have found some fresh angles on prayer in these pages that might suggest ways round some of your own stumbling blocks, or encourage you to try some new stepping stones.

Two of the most commonly experienced problems in prayer are explored in this last section: the problem of distraction, and the vexed question of whether God really answers prayer. And some stepping stones are introduced: the gift of companionship in prayer, whether individual or in community; some suggestions for keeping a spiritual journal, and the grace that awaits us if we look beyond the fences we tend to erect around ourselves and listen to those who live 'beyond the pale'.

Finally, was St Paul really serious when he urged us 'to pray at all times'? Decide for yourself whether prayer can become a way of life so natural that it informs every moment of our being.

21. Distractions, diversions, destinations
Learning to focus

22. Is God deaf?
Does God answer prayer?

23. Companions and community
Walking with a soul-friend; praying with the Church

24. Teach yourself patchworking
Keeping a spiritual journal

25. Beyond the pale
Learning from beyond the margins

26. Prayer unceasing?
Letting prayer become a way of life

21. DISTRACTIONS, DIVERSIONS, DESTINATIONS

Learning to focus

However incompetent we may all feel ourselves to be in the art of praying, when it comes to distractions, we can nearly all grade ourselves as experts.

The question is asked over and over again: 'How can I stay with prayer and free myself of the endless queue of distractions?'

Perhaps you remember when we first began this journey into prayer, and looked at the need for inner stillness, the image of a stormy sea proved helpful in revealing that at only a relatively small depth below the trough of the highest wave, there would be stillness. The big problem with our inner 'waves' is that what is happening on the surface *seems* so very much more real and insistent than what is happening deep down. Now that we have looked at the possibility of a deep contemplative prayer that is active in the depths of us, while we think nothing is going on at all, it becomes easier to see that our distractions in prayer are operating on the surface, and this is why they seem to dominate us so much and claim our attention so insistently.

There is, of course, no cast-iron solution to the problem of distractions in prayer. If there were, someone would surely have patented it by now, and we would all be queuing up to acquire it. But a couple of general guidelines may be helpful.

Ignore the attention-seekers ...

When distractions come, remember that they are actually only bobbing on the surface of your prayer, and they do not have the power to deflect you from your course, unless you choose to *give* them that power. You might compare it with driving a car, and thinking, as you drive, continually about your destination and how much you are looking forward to arriving.

During the course of the journey all kinds of things may happen. It may begin to rain, and you have to fiddle with the windscreen wipers. The radio programme may start to bore you, so you have to re-tune to another station. The children may be squabbling in the back seat. The road may be up, and you may have to follow a diversion. Or the tyre might blow, and you have to change it. All these things can be incredibly annoying and time wasting, and can really set you on edge, but in the evening, when you are relaxing at your destination, you will hardly remember them. I think distractions are like that, and should not be given more importance than they deserve. Instead of attending to them, focus on the 'ten feet down' approach. Acknowledge the disturbance, but keep returning to your deeper sense of the 'destination', which is to be close to God and your own deepest centre.

... but look after the genuine calls

Some of the apparently trivial distractions in prayer are worth dealing with when they arise, because they won't go away. These are things like: 'Did I turn the gas off?' 'Is the baby safe?' Such matters are easy to deal with and they *must* be dealt with, because you will certainly not come to inner peace until you have resolved them. Sometimes the phone rings during my prayer, and, because I have no idea whether the call is important or not, I have to answer it. So I just apologise to God, as to a friend, and ask him to excuse me for a minute. Then I let it go, and come back to prayer when I can, without any unnecessary agonising, which would be another distraction, of course!

A friend once gave me two very helpful and encouraging pieces of advice about distractions. She reminded me that, though I feel as if I have been distracted fifty times in half an hour of prayer, it is equally true that I have also turned back to God fifty times as well, and such a conversion record is no bad thing.

Her other piece of wisdom was borrowed from Luther, who said: 'Distractions are like birds flying round your head. You can't stop them flying, but you don't have to let them build nests in your hair.' What this is really saying is that if you keep your eyes on the road, then the swipe of the windscreen wipers won't have the power to make you go off course.

To this I would just add one piece of advice of my own:

Distractions are not sins. They are not a matter for confession. The guilt they generate is a false guilt, and a further distraction. Don't let it tie you up in its knots.

When is a distraction not a distraction?

Sometimes, however, our distractions can be trying to tell us something. If a particular distraction just won't let you go, it can be worthwhile to take it on board and ask God to show you where it is pointing. In effect, you are taking your 'distraction' into prayer, and it may be that when you do this, the distraction will actually become part of the destination because it has its roots in something that needs your prayerful attention.

A friend once shared with me his experience of trying to pray in a quiet chapel in a retreat house. He was facing a big redundancy programme at his place of work and was justifiably anxious about his future. But he had come to the retreat house in the hope of putting these anxieties aside for a while. As he sat quietly praying in the chapel, a cleaner arrived on the scene with her vacuum cleaner. She worked her way noisily round the chapel, and he found himself becoming more and more frustrated. Eventually she unplugged the machine and started to move off. He breathed a sigh of relief and looked forward to the return of silence. But just before she left, she came up alongside him and tapped his shoulder. He started up at the unexpected interruption, and then she spoke: 'Can you turn the lights out, luv, when you go?'

In spite of himself, he had to smile at the way her words had bounced into his attempts at prayer, and then the external distraction of her presence turned into what appeared to be an internal distraction. He suddenly remembered a joke poster that had been put up on the office wall: 'Will the last person to leave please turn out the lights!' And with that, the whole issue of redundancy, which he had been suppressing, came flooding back all over him, as he prayed there, but now it was gently relieved by the touch of lightness, and the wry smile over the remembered poster. He was able to bring it openly and honestly to God in his prayer, and during the evening that followed, he felt able to share it with others, and find new ways forward in dealing with his anxieties.

So don't throw your distractions away too readily. You may be throwing good prayer out along with them.

A lorry has shed its load . . .

These words, coming through on the car radio, can raise the hairs on the back of your neck like nothing else. In our family this usually means a scrambled rummage for the road map, accompanied by impatient admonitions to half-asleep passengers to search for a suitable diversion route, and a spot of bad temper all round.

I recall a trip we once made across northern Europe, along the German autobahn system. A tedious journey at the best of times, but that day the autobahn was full, and the standing traffic tailed back for miles. Fortunately, salvation was at hand. The German system of diversions was also in place and we slipped off at the next junction, and followed the diversion number, to arrive back on the autobahn, having by-passed the obstruction, at the next following junction. A trivial incident, but it taught me something about distractions.

I noticed that while we were driving round the diversion route we lost all sense of the real journey. Suddenly we were not on a clear, straight, road any more, but winding our way through all kinds of towns and villages that we never planned to visit! In such a situation we can easily become preoccupied with these new minor visions, which may either delight us or depress us, and if we had stopped to take our bearings at any point, we would have thought we were travelling in all kinds of 'wrong' directions. All too easy then to panic, and think you have lost your way.

- While you are off on the 'diversion', you lose sight, temporarily, of your destination.
- The diversion does what its name suggests: it diverts your energy away from the real journey. On the motorway this energy is measured in litres of fuel. On our inner journey it is our vital spiritual energy which is being expended.
- But if you follow the diversion signs or numbers, you will eventually arrive back on the right road.

The power of a piece of thread

What form might these diversion signs take in our prayer? I think I tend to see them as a kind of Ariadne's thread. Ariadne, in classical mythology

The only compass you can trust is your deep desire for the destination.

helped Theseus to find his way out of the Labyrinth by giving him a ball of string with which he could retrace his steps. The German diversion numbers on the side roads are exactly like that. They provide a ball of string to bring you back to where you want to be. When I lose myself in distractions and diversions in prayer, I often find that a marker like this can help me to get back. I might, for example, need to go back to read the Scripture passage I started with, or I might hold a particular phrase, or mantra, in my mind. When you are on the diversion route, there are no signs to your real destination. The only guide you have are the diversion signs or numbers themselves, and your knowledge of the overall map. On your inner journey the only compass you can trust is the deep desire in your heart for that destination towards which you are travelling.

After the Second World War many thousands of people in Europe were displaced, and became homeless refugees trekking across the continent. One such person is Hanna. She is well into middle age now, but at the time she was a twelve-year-old schoolgirl. When the Soviet troops moved into her home town in Silesia, now part of Poland, she and her family became homeless. Her mother remained behind with the youngest child, a two-year-old. Her father and brother managed to stay together but were interned in a refugee camp. Hanna, alone and with no possessions, started to walk. All she had was an address of a relative many hundreds of miles away in the far west of Germany. She walked. And she walked. And somehow or other she kept on walking, week after week, month by month, until she finally arrived. What kept her walking? No doubt there were plenty of 'distractions' in the form of threats to her safety or temptations to give up and let herself fall into despair. What kept her going was that address in her pocket, of the place, far away, where she would be welcomed and received. There was no energy to visit all the side-shows on the way. She needed every ounce of energy just to keep going.

And so do we! And we, too, need to keep our fingers curled round that 'address in our pockets' which reminds us every passing moment that our destination is with God and that this is where our whole desire is focused, however interesting the diversions may become.

Yet, returning to the motorway, there really *was* an obstruction and it really was necessary to make the diversion. Perhaps much of our experience of feeling lost and distracted is just this – our energies are being deflected because an obstruction has to be got past. Like the waters of a river trying to find a way round a boulder or a fallen tree. I've never seen a river cry because it had to flow round a complication, and couldn't go straight to the ocean homing. So why do I? And God's guiding is so much like the German diversion systems: if I follow the right number – my inner compass – my Ariadne's thread – it *will* bring me back to the straight road, after the obstruction has been circumvented!

Moving, swiftly, from classical mythology to modern technology, I must report that while I have been writing this chapter, I have been distracted:

• By a huge thud that could have been something serious and had to be investigated, just in case, and turned out to be a pigeon that had flown into the upstairs window.

- By a letter that required me to reply to it and send off a parcel before the post office closed.
- By a failure of my e-mail system that forced me to make an urgent phone call to get it back on line, in order to receive a message I need to have for a meeting tomorrow.
- And so on . . . .

Yet the focus of my morning has remained on the task of writing this chapter. My Ariadne's thread is the fact that the page I am working on has stayed faithfully on my computer screen, and the little black cursor has even stayed at the word where I left off. And the desire that keeps me going – and keeps me coming back! – is the overriding desire to share these thoughts with you, which has the power to attract me more even than the poor pigeon or the e-mail system's indigestion. I don't feel guilty because I have attended to these other things in between. They had to be done. And I don't even feel unduly frustrated, because my firm intention to write this chapter has not been permanently undermined by these diversions. And I feel that my prayer is like that too. The 'page' of my focus on God remains open on my heart's 'screen', even if my mind and body are at the back door, burying the pigeon's body. And the 'cursor' of my deeper level of attentiveness never leaves the point where my heart is 'parked'. And my desire for communion with God in prayer is, in the end, strong enough to keep me coming back.

The toy magnet challenges Isaac Newton

Finally, in case you are still worried about the power your distractions seem to have to divert your attention and destroy the focus of your prayer, try thinking of your heart's inner journey in terms of an iron filing being drawn steadily and reliably home to a vast magnet that we might call the heart of God. This is as sure and certain as the fact that we are held on earth by the power of gravity. We don't spend time worrying in case gravity fails and we suddenly float off into space. As far as our minds and understanding can tell, there is absolutely no danger of the laws of gravity breaking down. It is equally certain (so we say with our lips) that the love of God holds us in being in a way that will never let us go, whatever we do or fail to do.

But . . . you can override the laws of gravity with a pocket magnet that any child can buy for fifty pence in Woolworths. You can pick up a pin from the floor and force it *temporarily* to defy gravity. This thought used to depress me. I could see in it the potential inherent in my distractions and addictions to pull me off course, and draw me away from my journey with God. Until I realised one morning in a liberating shaft of clarity, that the pocket magnet, together with everything it can attract to itself, is itself held to earth by the law of gravity.

And in the same way, I believe, all our distractions and all the things that have the power to distract us are likewise held, themselves, in the magnetic field of God who is infinitely larger than all the distractions that ever were, are or shall be.

Likewise, the ocean of God 'in whom we live and move and have our being' is deeper and more vast than the passing disturbance that makes waves on the surface of our consciousness. On this we can depend.

TAKING IT FURTHER . . .

A colleague of mine, who also, in his spare time, taught children to play the violin, once told me that the worst thing you can do with children you are trying to teach is to tell them to 'Concentrate!' As soon as they begin to 'concentrate', they are concentrating on the art of concentration, and no longer on the art of playing the violin. It made good sense to me, and not just in the field of music!

So the worst thing I could suggest, by way of an exercise, is anything that focuses your attention on your 'distractions'. The only thing that helps distractions is to focus on the *destination*, and to ignore the distractions as far as is humanly possible. So a more sensible exercise might be simply: Now forget this chapter and move on!

However, there is something that can help us to see our 'distractions' in perspective, and that, ironically, is to 'magnify' them and make them life-size.

To do this, try drawing a little sketch of the path your life has taken so far. Notice its main direction. Where have your desires, your dreams, your energies been mainly invested? How might you describe your desired destination in this journey? Let this become the 'main road' in your picture.

Now just notice the various side tracks you have taken. What were they about? Where did they lead you? Did you go down those tracks in order to circumvent some perceived obstruction or block or difficulty in your life? Are there any cul-de-sacs along the way? Did you get stuck there, or did you find your way out? How do you feel now about the shape of your journey? Whatever convolutions it displays, it has nevertheless brought you to where you are today. How does that make you feel?

If any of these questions draws your attention particularly, just stay with it, and let it lead you to a deeper understanding of the relative power of your distractions vis-à-vis your real journey.

When your mind and thoughts are 'all over the place', and you feel, as John Milton once wrote, that 'chaos is come again', call to mind what God did with the first primeval chaos (Genesis 1:1–2). Ask him, quite simply and trustfully, to let his Spirit hover over your personal chaos. Surrender the task of creation back into his hands.

This may not immediately reveal a solution, but it will draw your heart down towards its tap root in him, leaving your troubled distractedness up on the surface where the storm will blow itself out in its own time. It will take you to the place of calm where you will be able to see the real issues involved.

Yesterday, last week, last month, you struggled with a bout of distraction in your prayer. (If this isn't true for you it certainly is for me!) Can you remember what that distraction was about? What does that tell you about the permanence of its power over you?

22. IS GOD DEAF?

Does God answer prayer?

This is a difficult question that confronts all of us from time to time. Does God really hear our prayer? Why doesn't he appear to keep his promise to give us all we ask, if we only believe? Many a fervent Christian's faith has been sorely tested when heartfelt prayer, for example to make a sick person well again, has not been answered in any way that we can recognise.

Maybe the pictures of the cartwheel and the potter's wheel from Chapter 19 can help us move a little closer to that mystery surrounding the way God does, or (more often) does not appear to *answer* our prayer . . . . I would just invite you to let these wheels adjust your *focus* a little.

When you think of the spinning wheel, the centre of gravity, the hub of the activity, is at the centre. Our whole universe spins around an invisible centre of gravity, just as the cartwheel turns about its hub and the potter's wheel spins around its spindle. The rim of the cartwheel, just as the clay on the potter's wheel, can only see the view from the edge. It needs the potter's eyes to know what all the motion is leading to. It takes the driver of the cart to know where the wheels are moving to. We are living, consciously, all the time on that outer edge of God's creating, redeeming work in his creation. It should not surprise us, therefore, that we can't very often see what he is about!

If you imagine the clay, feeling the pressure of the potter's hands and the dizziness of the spinning, you will see how meaningless it would be for the clay to make judgements about how well the pot is working out.

And if you imagine the cartwheel running over rough ground or bogged down in the mud, it might well think the journey had ended in disaster, but the driver of the cart knows better. We ourselves, especially as parents, often have to deny our children the little things they ask for in order to give them more truly what they need and what will draw them forward to a fuller, healthier, happier life. If God seems deaf to you, try adjusting your focus away from the little bit of reality you can see from your position on the edge of all the motion and commotion, and reminding yourself that you are in the hands of the One who alone can see the Wholeness of his creation.

The song of the caged bird

A friend recently lent me the video of *The Robe*, which tells a story of how Jesus' seamless robe, gambled for by the soldiers when he was crucified, might have gone on to affect its 'owner' in powerful and disturbing ways, until that owner was eventually drawn into a new faith.

One of the most moving incidents portrayed in this film is the meeting with Miriam, a crippled woman in the village of Cana. Miriam had been a crippled young girl at the time of Jesus' first miracle in Cana at the wedding feast, and she describes how she alone, of all the villagers, had not attended this wedding because it was too painful for her to face the fact that in her crippled state she would never be a bride herself. As the villagers had left her that day, to go to the wedding, she had been enclosed in her own bitterness and pain. When they returned they found her singing. No less a cripple, physically, than before, she had nevertheless been miraculously healed. Her crippled heart had been made whole. The wings of her heart had taken flight and shown themselves to be infinitely more powerful than the cage of disability that contained her. She was transformed.

When Marcellus, the Roman tribune who 'owned' the Robe, challenged her with the taunt that Jesus had not, after all, answered her prayer for a cure for her crippled body, she admitted that this same thought had troubled her too for many years. Surely the Lord who had freed her heart could have given her back the use of her body? But slowly, as the years passed, she became increasingly aware of a great gift concealed in her handicapped life. Remaining a cripple, for all to see, she had nevertheless experienced the heights of her own soul's flight. Had she been physically healed, she realised, she would have been just a 'special case', a seven-day wonder perhaps, but not a woman with whom other women could identify. Remaining a cripple, on the other hand, had made her a kind of gateway to God for all other cripples – a living testimony to the possibility of singing one's heart's song while enclosed in a crippling cage.

Just a story, of course. But perhaps you know someone like Miriam.

The wings of your heart are stronger
than all the cages that contain you.

Someone whom God seems unwilling to 'cure', but who has become a special messenger of his grace in ways that would not have been possible otherwise. A 'wounded healer'. Perhaps you are such a person yourself? Perhaps, amid all the confusion of your 'unanswered' prayers, there is a caged bird singing in your heart, singing a Gospel song that resonates in other people's lives in ways that you may never be aware of.

I have a friend who is blind. Not only that, but his life has been blighted in many other ways, through the blows of history, war, persecution and family break-up. He finds his blindness very hard to bear. It seems to defy faith and prayer, with its heartrending 'Why, Lord? *Why?*' God could have cured him, surely, but had he done so there are countless classes of small children in a local school for the blind in our town who would never have had the hugely healing experience of sitting around him in their class-rooms, week by week, year by year, listening to his stories, hearing his gentle, confidence-inspiring voice, learning from him about blindness *from the inside*. These children have learned to trust him, and, through him, to trust themselves in a dangerous world. And we, his sighted friends, have learned from him that insight (which he has in abundance) is an even more precious gift than sight. And so a deeper purpose has been fulfilled than our partial prayers could ever have formulated.

A wand or a spear?

I get very frustrated when the Christian churches seem to seduce people into expecting a wave of a divine magic wand to answer their prayers and fulfil their desires, without encouraging them to go deeper and deeper until they discover the *real* roots of those prayers and desires in their hearts. It seems to me that this is the very opposite of how things work. The Good News is not that God will 'fix' us with his wand, but rather that, when life 'fixes' us with its spear, that spear will, paradoxically, open up a flow of grace within us which will be seen to be the same living stream as the flow of our own deepest desire.

The wand, if it existed, might satisfy the lesser wants and wishes with which we sometimes bombard God in our prayers, but the spear is the way to the deepest stream. This is what released the stream that flowed from Jesus' pierced side on Calvary, and still flows from our broken hearts and broken lives.

When the jigsaw is complete, we will find, so I believe, that God has been answering the prayers we have not yet found the words to express. We will discover that he has all along been fulfilling the deepest desires of our hearts that are still unacknowledged by us because they lie buried under layers of lesser wants and wishes. Perhaps our simplest, and most sincere prayer might be that he will open our eyes to become aware, more and more, of the deepest longings of our own hearts, that he is continually seeking to fulfil. Perhaps it isn't so much that God is deaf, as that we ourselves are still blind to what we truly long for.

Missing the obvious

It's a well-known phenomenon that writers never see their own mistakes in their scripts, which is why scripts always have to be proof-read by someone unfamiliar with the text, who will read what is actually there, and not what he expects to be there. The writer will invariably see what he intended to write. The proof-reader will read what was actually written. And it is amazing just how many mistakes a proof-reader will pick up, even though the writer was sure that he had checked and double-checked it.

Prayer is like that too perhaps. We don't see God's answers to our prayers, because our minds are completely tuned in to what we *expect* him to do, or even, dare I say, what we, in our wisdom, have *instructed* him to do. And our own expectation represents a very small waveband indeed, when set against the whole cosmic range of God's possibilities. Thus it becomes very easy to miss the obvious, because we are waiting for events to unfold as we had planned them, and we are blind to the ways in which God is *actually* active in the situation.

This blindness can be exacerbated even more if, deep down, we don't *want* any solution to the problem other than the one we have worked out for ourselves. I remember once giving God very detailed instructions about how to solve a particular problem. I had worked it all out for him. All he needed to do was put his signature to it and get on with it. Imagine my chagrin, therefore, when he delivered a completely different solution, that I could never, in my wildest dreams, have thought up, and one which caused me personally considerable discomfort!

A way to move beyond this kind of habitual blockage is to try turning your prayer on its head. Instead of focusing on what you are asking God to do in your life, and then waiting to see whether he does it, try noticing what he is *actually* doing in your life, and reflecting on how that is revealing his unceasing engagement with your deepest desires.

As so often in prayer, the key is in the *focus*. Look again at the two situations above – I don't *see* God's answers, or I don't *want* God's answers:

- Often we fail to see God's answers to our prayers because our focus is on our own expectations rather than on his limitless power to move our hearts closer to their own fulfilment
- If we are praying for others, but don't want any answers that we haven't invented ourselves, the focus is surely on ourselves, and on the satisfaction of our pride in 'doing good', and not on the real needs and desires of the person we are praying for.

We might experience a radically different perspective on things if we could ask instead:

'What is God doing right now, in my daily life (or in the life of the person I am praying for)?'

If we can trust God to be doing what is most deeply in conformance with the deepest desires of ourselves, of each other and of the whole of creation, then we may see answers to prayers that we had never dared to hope for.

An inside job?

In Chapter 9 we looked at the possibility that God might answer our prayers for others by asking us to answer them ourselves – by challenging us to become the answers to our own prayers.

Part of the power of prayer, it seems to me, is to awaken our own hearts (not God's!) to what lies at the root of our desires or the core of our needs. Once this awakening has happened, in any particular issue or concern, this may be a signal to turn the dreaming into action. Perhaps any prayer that we make should be offered on the assumption that we ourselves are at least on the short list of candidates for the job of answering it in practical ways.

This assumption is worth examining, whether the prayer was for someone else or for something in our own lives. Praying for success in an examination is not likely to be answered unless we invest some effort ourselves. That much is obvious. But what, for example, when it comes to praying for issues of social justice. We may beg God to convert the hearts and minds of our leaders, but what choices do we make in practice, when we vote, or when we come up against unfair or unjust behaviour on our doorstep or in our own families?

Perhaps there are a few questions we need to ask ourselves, when we reflect on our prayer:

- In what practical ways might I personally begin to answer this prayer?
- Do I really want this prayer to be answered, and am I willing to leave the form of the answer entirely to God?
- How much am I prepared to pay (in money, time, energy, patience, good will) to bring about an answer to this prayer? Which doesn't mean 'bribing' God to do things our way, but counting, and willingly committing, the cost in personal terms of co-operating with God on the issue we are praying about.

That we might see . . .

In St Luke's Gospel (Chapter 18:35–43 and Chapter 19:1–10) two stories are told side by side. Both are about people who wanted 'to see'.

The first, a blind beggar on the roadside near Jericho, heard a crowd going past, and asked what all the fuss was about. They told him that Jesus was passing by. When he heard this news he made up his mind to seize the opportunity to beg Jesus for help. He called out to him, but the crowd tried to silence him. Undeterred, he shouted all the louder. Jesus heard the cries and stopped, asking for the man to be brought to him, and then asked him: 'What do you want me to do for you?' 'Lord, that I might see . . .!' he begged. 'Let me see again.' And the man's sight was restored. We are told that he then followed Jesus, praising God, and that all those who saw the effects of the miracle were similarly drawn to praise God.

The second person, Zacchaeus, had a different kind of blindness. He was quite simply too short to see over the heads of the crowd. Desperate to catch a glimpse of Jesus, he climbed a tree to gain a better view. That might have been the end of the matter, but Jesus noticed Zacchaeus up the tree and stopped at that very spot, peered up at him and called him into something far beyond what he had hoped for — or felt himself ready for. 'Zacchaeus, come down. Hurry, because I am to stay at your house today.' This turn of events caused an outbreak of complaint among the crowd.

Zacchaeus was a notorious sinner, a senior tax official who had lined his pockets with their money. Perhaps he regretted the sudden sweep of the searchlight that his perch in the tree had brought upon him. The price of 'seeing' was 'being seen'. There, in the presence of the burning integrity of the Lord, he had no choice but to acknowledge the truth about himself that the searchlight had exposed. It was his conversion experience. The searchlight of truth became his light on the road to Damascus. The story ends with Jesus' words of loving, healing acceptance: 'This man too is a son of Abraham.' It was the turn of the crowd, now, 'to see'. It was no longer possible, simply to demonise those parts of God's creation that they did not like. Like Zacchaeus, they too had come out to see the Lord, and like him, they went home having been challenged to 'see themselves'.

I think that these two stories can give us some insight into the nature of our prayer and how God might answer it:

• Nothing clarifies our minds so much as raw need. The blind beggar knew exactly what he wanted. Lacking almost everything except life itself, he focused his whole attention on the one thing that he knew would change his life. Prayer that comes from such need seems to bring us straight to the heart of God. When we bring our needs to God, are we not in reality begging him for that one thing that will change our lives? And will we recognise it when it is given? Will we trust God's judgement, or our own, as to what that 'one thing' really is?

• What effort are we willing to make to open ourselves up to God's answers? The blind beggar had to overcome the hostility of the crowd, and keep on persisting, until he caught the Lord's ear. How do we score on the persistence scale? Zacchaeus made the effort to climb a tree. How far will we go to meet the Lord?

• The answer to prayer can sometimes turn the prayer on its head. We ask 'to see' and we find ourselves 'being seen'. Prayer turns out to be a blank cheque. Are we really willing to sign that cheque and hand it over, unconditionally, to the Lord?

• Prayer may be solitary and individual, but the answer affects the whole community. Everyone was caught up in praise following the healing of the blind beggar. Everyone found themselves under the searchlight of truth when Zacchaeus made his bid 'to see'. God's action in the life of each one of us is action in the life of all his creation. We are affected by the answers to each other's prayers. Are our prayers just about 'me' (perhaps at the expense of others), or are they about the needs of all his family? If God responds to the desires I have in my own little world, how will this response affect those around me? No caring parent would give one child in the family something that would harm or deprive the other siblings.

Perhaps, then, instead of bombarding God with requests for 'what is not', we might try, instead, asking him to open our eyes to see what IS.

TAKING IT FURTHER . . .

The other day I heard a story in a homily. The preacher said he had heard it on the radio, and believed it to be a true story of a man's conversion experience. Wherever it comes from, I thank its unknown author.

A rich American business tycoon was driving through a very poor part of town one day in his huge new Cadillac. He parked it, to attend to some business, and when he came back a street urchin was peering into it. Thinking the boy was up to no good, he challenged him, but the boy just gazed at him, with awe-filled eyes, and asked: 'How much did it cost you?'

'I don't know', he replied, a little nonplussed.

'How come that you don't know?' the urchin went on. 'How can you have a car like that and not know how much it cost?'

'Well, actually, my brother bought it for me', the man answered. 'He gave it to me.'

The boy was astounded. He was silent for a moment, and then, thinking aloud, he began:

'My, I wish I could . . ..'

Mentally the man finished the sentence for him: 'I wish I could have a brother like that.'

But the boy spoke out his heart's wish rather differently:

'My, I wish I could be a brother like that!'

It was a sentence that changed the life of the man who heard it. It was a modern miracle of sight restored and of poverty found to hold eternal riches.

How do you feel about this story? When you look back over your prayers, are they about 'having', or 'being'? Do you think it makes a difference?

Take some time to reflect on where you feel God has been active in your life during, say, the past year. How has this action been fulfilling deep desires within you? Can you see any connections between these deep desires, which God has been attending to, and the prayers you have been expressing explicitly?

I remember going through a very short 'phase' as an adolescent when I longed to have an electric train set. One day, just before Christmas, my father came home with a parcel wrapped in paper from our local electrical goods shop, and I was so thrilled that my dream might be close to coming true. But on Christmas Day I unwrapped not a train set, but an electric blanket! We lived in a cold, badly insulated house, and the nights came when I was so thankful for a warm bed. But at the moment of unwrapping I was hardly able to conceal my disappointment. Yet my parents had the longer, wiser view. They knew that my obsession with trains was fleeting, but that my need for warmth would always be there. They gave me what I really needed, not what I wanted.

Look back over some of your life's disappointments. With hindsight, did you find that any grace or blessing flowed out of that time of disappointment, that perhaps could not have reached you otherwise?

23. COMPANIONS AND COMMUNITY

*Walking with a soul-friend; praying with the
Church*

The journey into prayer – the inner journey of our hearts towards our
eternal reality – can sometimes seem a very lonely one. There are times in
most of our lives when we feel very isolated in our spiritual searching.
Perhaps there are experiences we long to share with another 'kindred
spirit'. But kindred spirits are not exactly thick on the ground, and when
we most need them they are often at their most elusive. And maybe there
are times when we feel we are going round in circles, or even going off
course, yet so often we have no way of checking things out with another
person who knows the reality of the inner journey and takes our searching seriously. Worst of all, perhaps, there are times when we may doubt the
authenticity of our own experience, because we know very well that most
of the people around us in our daily lives would think we had flipped, if
we were to reveal the depths of our prayer, and the central place in our
hearts of our relationship with God.

I would like to suggest that there are two gifts in our lives, waiting to be
claimed, which are given precisely to hold us in our lonely journeying, and
to restore our certainty that we are not amputated limbs, but vital cells of
a living Body. One is the gift of spiritual companionship with a fellow
believer with whom we can share something of the experience of our
journeying. The other is the gift of community with the whole Body of
Christ in his Church.

Anam Cara – friend of my journey

Since the beginnings of the emergence of human consciousness, men and
women have expressed a sense of quest, journey, pilgrimage in their
searching for the meaning and the direction of their lives. 'Rites of passage'
in every form of human society, assert our sense of life as journey. We see,
for example, how in many cultures the dead seem always to have been sent

on their onward journey with tokens of what they would need for the way – food, money, precious vessels and so on. Sometimes they have been despatched on board a boat, loosed from their earthly moorings to make the journey home to their eternal reality. And if you think that this is just a relic from the past, have you never heard a comment, after a funeral, such as, 'Well he had a good send-off.'

This deep awareness of life as a journey eventually became formalised into the world's great religions – the journey of the soul towards Nirvana in Buddhism, the exodus journey from slavery to freedom that underlies Judaism and Islam, and the People of the Way, who were the first Christians.

Our own Christian journeying, especially in these islands, was formed by the powerful Celtic sense of life as a pilgrimage, and it is from the Celts that we have the expression *anam cara*, which means 'soul-friend'. In the Celtic Christian communities, a soul-friend was a person with whom you could share your journey – someone who would *listen*, without any judgement, but with unconditional love, and, as it were, hold up for you a mirror of your searching, so that you would be able to see for yourself something of the inner movements of your heart. Together, then, you would be able to discern the ways in which God seemed to be drawing you, which might include times when your soul-friend would challenge and confront you with the demands of your own inner truth.

A soul-friend, in Celtic times, had no special qualifications, except the one overriding requirement to be a person of prayer, someone who was taking their own spiritual journey seriously, someone who loved God. Soul-friends could be either male or female and were frequently lay people with no status in the Church. It was a ministry in which 'ordinary' believers could accompany one another on The Way. It was also a ministry which was so highly valued that it was said that 'a person without a soul-friend is like a body without a head'.

The gift of soul friendship, then, is part of our Celtic heritage. And the good news is that this ministry is available to us today, in ever-increasing measure. The Christian Church is reclaiming the charism of soul friendship in all kinds of ways. Some call it 'accompanying the journey', or 'spiritual companionship' or 'mentoring' or 'spiritual direction'. This last term, however, is misleading, because a soul-friend does *not* 'direct'. God alone, through his Holy Spirit, is the one who guides the pilgrim, and the soul-friend simply walks alongside, listening with inner ears and giving the support of friendship, as the pilgrim lives out the promptings of God's call.

How do you find a soul-friend? It may seem like a daunting challenge if you embark on it 'cold'. You are, after all, hoping for a companion with whom you can be completely open about your innermost life, someone you can trust completely to hold all that you share in total confidentiality, and someone you feel personally at ease with. The first step, if you are looking for such a person, is to look, prayerfully, around your own circle of friends and fellow believers. Is there anyone among them who might feel 'right' for this very special kind of relationship? Is there someone who is 'on your wavelength', who has the gift of being able to listen with complete and loving attention, *without imposing their own 'agenda' on you*? This last point is important. The relationship is, in a sense, one-way. The pilgrim shares, and the soul-friend listens. Most people seem to find this the most effective way of 'sharing the journey', and of course it follows that anyone ministering to another as a soul-friend will themselves have a soul-friend too, with whom they share their own journey.

Because so many people find themselves, from time to time, lost and alone on their inner journey, gradually networks of pilgrims have evolved around the country, and indeed around the world, to help individuals find contact with other journeyers. Mostly these networks have sprung out of the needs people have actually felt for this kind of companionship. They have never been, and never can be, imposed 'from above', but have grown up 'from below'. They are a potent sign of the desire for growth at the grass-roots level, and it is at the grass roots of communities of believers that the need is being addressed. An increasing number of Christians, both lay and ordained, now seek training in the basic listening skills to enable them to be alongside others in this way, and almost certainly there will be such 'prayer guides' or 'companions' somewhere in your area. There is a contact address at the end of this book to which you can write for more details of any networks like this in your area.

A relationship with a soul-friend will provide the space for the two of you to meet regularly, perhaps every few weeks or so, for you to talk about what seems to have been happening in your relationship with God and in your prayer. You are completely free to say as much or as little as you wish. Your soul-friend will know how to be present to your silences and to your tears, as well as to your words and your rejoicing.

Some people share their journey with a few friends in a faith-sharing group. You may find such a group in your church or neighbourhood, or, if there is none, you may feel drawn to start one. I know of one group of people who meet each Friday morning when they have taken their young children to school. They gather for an hour in a room in the school and bring a powerful presence of prayer into the life of that school, as well as giving each other much-needed support in their personal relationships with God.

When we share our journey, either one-to-one or in a group, or both, we are participating in a special way in what St Paul calls the long act of giving birth to Christ in his world. We are ministering to each other as midwives, tending each other's coming to life and growth, being present to each other's pain and fears, hopes and dreams, and sharing that moment of wonder when another person recognises God's presence in their hearts and their lives, and holds that new life in their arms, knowing it for what it really is.

Praying with the Church

I remember a warm morning in July, some years ago. We were visiting friends in the Czech Republic, and had followed the Moldau valley out of Prague, to share in the early morning Mass at the shrine of Swata Hora. The sun filtered warmly through the cloisters, and there was a peace there. It felt like the peace beyond the storm, and there had, indeed, been storms across this land, along this valley, during the course of its history.

The words of the Czech liturgy floated through my consciousness without touching my understanding. Indeed, my 'understanding' failed me here completely. I didn't understand a word of the liturgy, but I followed it closely, nonetheless, because I knew that I shared the faith of these believers at a level more deep than words.

The homily passed me by, like the streaming waters of the Moldau, and my thoughts took off in their own directions. I thought of the tower of Babel, and how humankind had tried to construct its own way to heaven, only to fall into fragmentation, so that nation could no longer speak to nation.

Yet there, in that peaceful place, something seemed to flow in the opposite direction, towards re-integration instead of fragmentation. Flowing downhill, following the contours, like a river, the prayers of these people flowed on endlessly into an ocean of love. Czech prayers, flowing through the centuries, like the Moldau. And for a short while my own prayers joined with theirs, a fleeting tributary that would disappear as quickly as it came.

Here, where my own understanding failed, I was in touch with the full strength and power of their faith, and I became a part of it. The stream of our prayer would change and re-define, ever so subtly, the landscape of this place, this people, this part of God's creation, just as the Moldau defines and shapes the valley through which it flows. I discovered in those people a strength and a faith that is rooted deep in the earth, and which sustained and sheltered me, a stranger there, yet not a stranger. Their presence beside me felt like a powerful, unseen current in the river of my prayer. Their strength, their fidelity to truth, their disarming humility flowed all around me and I was changed by it. And strengthened, immeasurably. And content to let my own faith flow into it, down to the sea.

Not all experiences of liturgy and church are as positive as this one, I realise. Yet this, surely, is part of what our life as 'church', as community, as the Body of Christ is about. For me, it needed the shock of being in a place where I understood not a word of the language, to bring home to me the power of that current of faith that carries the Church home to God, and to help me acknowledge my own tiny part in it.

It seems to me that to journey in isolation, believing that our *individual* pilgrimage is what it is all about, is dangerously close to the ethos of the Tower of Babel. We may feel that our personal prayer soars up to the heavens sometimes, but is it drawing us closer together as the People of the Way, or is it isolating us into a spiritual ivory tower? Always knowing ourselves to be, for better or for worse, just one cell of the Body, just one pilgrim among countless millions, past, present and to come, is both humbling and enormously strengthening. It resonates with the image of the river, flowing on, gathering its tributaries, forming and shaping the landscape, and seeking the ocean of its destination.

To pray with the Church is to be part of this river. We pray with the Church, of course, every time we share in its liturgy, and being aware that this is what we are doing can help us to make that shared prayer a time of power and grace rather than a time of dry obligation or empty ritual.

Another way of linking your personal prayer with the prayer of the whole Church, if your Christian tradition uses a set lectionary, is to incorporate the day's Scripture readings into your own prayer. You may find that this is an excellent starting place for the imaginative meditation or forms of scriptural prayer that we have explored in earlier chapters.

Some people choose to pray the Divine Office, which links them daily to the official 'prayer of the Church' used by all clergy and religious and many lay people. Be careful, however, not to let this become an achievement course that you feel you have to accomplish every day, and which could crowd out time for simple stillness before the Lord.

At its best, to pray with the Church, which includes the invisible communion of all believers, alive on earth or alive in heaven, is to slip into the stream of life which is flowing through history, through every tradition of faith and through all time and space. Each cell draws its life from its belonging to the Body. Alone, it is nothing more than an interesting, but ultimately lifeless specimen. There is no such thing as a solitary journey with God, because we are all one in him.

TAKING IT FURTHER . . .

Think about finding a soul-friend.

Do you have contact with any faith-sharing group? If not, would you like to? Is there such a group in your neighbourhood? If not, you might like to think about starting one, by inviting a few friends to meet and share together how they feel about their relationship with God.

Try attending a service in a Church tradition other than your own, and let the not-quite-familiar words and liturgy work on you refreshingly, reminding you that you are part of a universal Church, infinitely rich in its diversity, yet one in its longing and searching for God.

There is no such thing as a
solitary journey with God.

In the early morning, when the sun is rising, stop for a moment to remember the people to the east of us who have just come to the end of their day. Let them be present in your prayer. Receive from them, in your imagination, the 'baton' of prayer, which you will carry forward, as a member of the universal Church, through the coming hours of light and activity. In the evening, as the light fades, remember the people to the West of us, who are just waking to the new day. In your imagination, pass on the 'baton' of prayer to them, and remember them in your prayers.

24. TEACH YOURSELF PATCHWORKING

Keeping a spiritual journal

Have you ever kept a diary?

Have you ever made a scrapbook?

Have you ever written a love letter?

Have you ever been spring-cleaning or decorating, and come across an old letter or newspaper or photograph, and found yourself re-living times and feelings long past?

Have you ever looked back on a memorable experience and thought to yourself: 'I wish I could freeze this moment!'?

I suspect that most people would answer 'Yes' to at least one of these questions. If you are one of them, then you have already made your own tracks in the adventure of what is sometimes called *'journalling'*.

'Journalling' is a word used to describe the habit of keeping a record, usually, but not necessarily, like a diary, of what seems to be happening in our inner world. However, I don't find the word 'journalling' very helpful or inviting myself, even though I personally do rather a lot of it, and so perhaps I might introduce you to the subject in a slightly different way . . . .

In Chapter 7 I shared the memory of the patchwork quilt, made as a gift to a retiring head teacher by the children she had taught, in which each patch was made by an individual child. Every patch recalled for her a person whose life had touched her own in a unique and special way. Just by looking at her quilt, patch by patch, each memory could be recalled and re-lived. And the whole quilt reminded her that every child, whom she had laughed with, shouted at, encouraged and wept over, was a precious fragment in the story of her own journey through the world.

A journal is a bit like that. Like a collection of 'patches', each recording, in perhaps quite different ways, a significant moment of our inner journey. Keeping a journal is a bit like collecting these patches and letting them accumulate into a quilt. Far from being a tedious chore, it can become an enjoyable, and a deepening, adventure, that we might simply call '*patch-working*'.

Patchworking is about the sort of things those opening questions were about. Reflecting on why we do those things can help us to see why patchworking can help our journeying.

- Why do we keep diaries or make scrapbooks or even take holiday photographs?
- Why do we write love letters or seek the depths of true companionship?
- Why do we spend more time reading the papers spread out on the floor than painting the walls?
- Why do we try to capture our 'magic moments'?

May I suggest a few answers:

We like to keep track of things, by recording our daily, weekly or monthly doings. Over time that gives us a sense that we are 'going somewhere' and not just drifting, even though such purpose is not usually obvious on the daily journey.

We like to look back on the high spots of our lives. This is more than just nostalgia. Re-living the times of special meaning and joy is like re-entering sacred space where we feel more 'real'. These are times when we have felt that we were 'living true' and they help us to trust that the signposts from the past are indicating a true direction for the future.

We need to pour out the deepest needs, feelings, longings of our hearts, as we might do in a love letter, or in a conversation with a loved and trusted friend.

I would suggest that, just as these are natural human instincts and desires, so too they are the motivation that might lead us to try out the possibilities of '*patchworking*', to discover more about the direction and the driving forces of our inner journey.

Let's consider a few examples. See whether any of these ways of looking at your journey strikes a chord with you.

A fly on the canvas . . .

Imagine a fly walking across a painting in the art gallery. It would see a very strange version of the picture. One stretch of the journey might be all red, the next might be all green, and there would appear to be no connection at all between the steps along the way. Until, of course, it flew off to perch on the opposite wall, and could suddenly see the picture as a whole. Then the 'red days' and the 'green days' would be seen as integral parts of the story. When we record the individual steps along our way, they seem to make very little sense. But if we can look back over a month, a year, a generation, we begin to see quite different patterns and meanings. We begin, imperfectly, to see our lives in the way that God sees them perfectly in all their fullness.

Mountains and molehills . . .

Most of us have faced obstacles on our life's journey that have seemed insuperable at the time. And most of us will remember niggling irritations that seemed trivial, yet which persisted in claiming our attention and were actually warning us about some deep-rooted and perhaps damaging movement taking shape in our lives. Time and distance help us to distinguish between the real mountains and the molehills along our journey, and prayerful reflection is the key to such discernment.

Words for the Way . . .

Many people feel that from time to time they are given 'messages' in prayer. For some this may be quite dramatic; for others the messages take the form of gentle suggestions from somewhere deep inside them. Two of my personal 'words' have been: 'Stay close to the spring' and 'Don't water the weeds'. They keep returning to me, and each time they go deeper. Words like this seem truly to come from God, and they are precious patches in our quilts.

The longest journey . . .

The word '*journal*' derives from the French word '*jour*', meaning '*day*', and so of course, does the word '*journey*'. Our story, mapped out in the patches of our quilt, is the record of a journey. It has been said that '*the longest journey is the journey from our heads to our hearts*', and that is precisely the route of the inner journey. Our patches are snapshots along that journey of risk, and discovery and joy.

Mr Craik and the inkblots . . .

Mr Craik was a school teacher in the days when children wrote with real
ink and books were meant to stay blot-free. The children in his class made
every effort to offer him unblemished homework, but often they failed. Mr
Craik could have pointed out these failings by ringing the ugly blots round
with his red pen and drawing attention to them with a reproachful ex-
clamation mark, as many of his colleagues did. But instead he took his own
pen and turned each sorrowful blot into an 'angel' by creating his own
little picture around it – a pretty face, a smiling sun, a dancing flower. Some
of the patches on our quilt will be blotted and spoiled. But God will turn
them into angels in ways that we will only discover if we go back to them
bravely over time, and see how they have been transformed into something
that will help us grow.

Unspoken conversations . . .

When I write down what is happening in my life and in my prayer I may
find that what appears on my 'patches' reveals areas of conflict and contra-
diction. You might say that my patches don't always have an easy neigh-
bourly relationship with one another, which shows me, in reality, that
different parts of me and my life are not very happily connected. When this
happens, it can be useful to let the conflicting elements hold a conversation with each other. This is sometimes called '*dialoguing*', but all it means
is allowing the different and opposed feelings and impulses within you to
have their say, within the shelter of your prayer. This can lead to a new
understanding of what is really, most importantly, going on inside you, and
how you can accept and receive what God is showing you of the oppo-
sitions in your heart. A journal is a good place in which to hold, and
record, this kind of inner conversation.

Samuel's new coat . . .

When Hannah gave her little son Samuel up to the service of God in the
Temple, she brought him a new coat every year, to replace the one he had
outgrown. God does the same with us, as he watches us growing in our love
of him and of our brothers and sisters. And nowhere is this more obvious

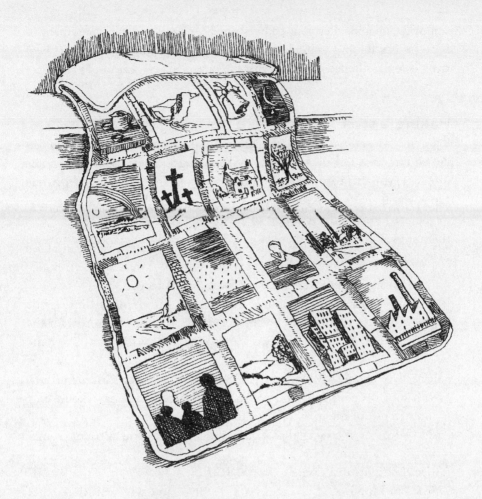

A quilt of experience,
stitched together with
the never~ending thread
of prayer.

than when you come to the end of a year's journal, or when you sew
together a collection of your patches. A new year is beginning, built on the
old and looking towards a future of surprises. A new book is a new coat for
the growing Samuel inside you, a space that you will grow into in ways you

cannot yet imagine. Let your patches observe God's first commandment to us, to be fruitful and multiply, until you can bring him your own quilt of many colours, stitched together with the never-ending thread of prayer.

Making a start

A journal can be in any form you like and it can contain whatever you feel like putting in it. The most usual way of keeping a journal is to take a note-book that you can easily carry around with you, and simply jot down the things you feel are speaking to you of your relationship with God and of your inner journey. These might include:

- Notes on what happens for you during times of prayer – anything God seems to be saying to you or asking of you – ways in which you notice how you respond to him and how he responds to you.
- Incidents or meetings or things that catch your attention during the course of your day. It can be very helpful to look out, each day, for the 'special moment or gift' that you want to thank God for particularly, and to make a note of it.
- Places where you have felt particularly at ease, close to God or in tune with your deepest reality. These are 'sacred spaces'. You may like to keep photographs of them, and return to them in prayer.
- Any 'words' or 'messages' that suggest themselves to you as having some-thing to say about your journey.
- Special insights that come to you.
- Highs and lows of your moods and feelings, and why you think they happened.
- Photographs, or just the names, of people who are significant in your life. These can remind you of what these people have given to you and act as prompts to remember them in your prayers
- Significant dreams; make a note of them immediately on waking if you can and record them just as they were, without trying to make sense of them.
- Notes or quotations from conversations, TV programmes, sermons, books, etc., that have come to life for you.
- The names of your 'angels' or 'wisdom figures', including any from the distant past. Try choosing the most important to you, and holding a

prayer conversation with them or writing a letter to them.

- Moments of panic, problems, crises or changes in your life, your deepest questions, doubts, fears, areas of pain. Express them freely. In doing so, you are also giving them to God, and you may be astounded, when you come to look back, how he has responded.
- Moments when God has touched you, and when you have felt really loved, encouraged, enlivened.

... In short, everything you notice as having deeper meaning for you, whether it appears to be 'good' or 'bad'. All these moments, incidents, experiences, feelings, reactions are patches for your quilt. Slow down, relax, re-play your day (or week, or month) and savour it. Notice its 'patches' and store them up for yourself in whatever way seems right for you, just as Mary stored up her memories of Jesus' childhood, and treasured them in her heart.

A few practicalities

- Don't ever let your 'patchworking' become a burden or a chore. There's no need to make a daily or weekly ritual of it and there's no need to feel it has to be 'properly written'. Just jot down whatever you feel is important to you. You are only writing for yourself.
- Date your entries. This can be quite important when you look back, and can help you make connections and trace the pattern of God's movement in your life.
- Keep your notebook handy. You'll find it's like a camera that you wish you had with you at unexpected moments. Don't let too much time go by before recording an important item; try to do it in the freshness of the moment.
- Try keeping a record of important times in your life, such as holidays, retreats, times of change and decision, even times of illness.
- Let the focus of what you do be not on yourself, but on what God is doing in you. 'Not I, but God in me!'
- Be completely honest. You are only writing for yourself and for God. If it helps, write down your thoughts and feelings in the form of letters to God, telling him exactly how things are with you. The privacy of your journal must be safeguarded. If you cannot be sure of this privacy, you might find it necessary to develop shorthand expressions or symbols to express your feelings, that only you will understand.

- Read back over your 'patches' at regular intervals and reflect on how you have grown from them. This helps you to focus on what God is doing in you, and it also helps to focus your thoughts on what you might want to share with your spiritual director or soul-friend.

Some 'Classic' Examples:

Dag Hammarskjöld *Markings*
Gerard W. Hughes SJ *In Search of a Way*
Berlie Doherty *Dear Nobody*
Thomas Merton *The Journals* (five volumes)
Anne Frank *The Diary of Anne Frank*
C. S. Lewis *A Grief Observed*
Dietrich Bonhoeffer *Letters and Papers from Prison*
Henri J. M. Nouwen *Sabbatical Journey*

And the finest example of all is of course the Old Testament, which is the journal of the human race and a patchwork quilt sewn together from the dreams and conflicts, the hopes and longings and betrayals, the angels and the inkspots of the whole human family.

25. BEYOND THE PALE

Learning from beyond the margins

We have almost come to the end of this beginning of an adventure into prayer. Where does the path lead from here on? Will our prayer remain just ours alone? Is our spiritual journey a solitary pilgrimage, undertaken in the hope of 'saving our own souls', or knowing ourselves more deeply? And if not – if we have come to recognise ourselves as journeying in *community* – what about those who have, apparently, no part in any such community of faith or of prayer? Does God ask us merely to sympathise with them, to shake the dust of their 'unfaith' off from our sandals and move on to where we, and our personal spirituality, find resonance and affirmation? Or does he challenge us in less comfortable ways?

Each of us must discern the answers in our own ways, but, before we part, I would like to introduce you to three people who have led me, in prayer and in life, 'beyond the pale' – across the margins that divide our 'respectable spirituality' from the hungry, aching world on the other side of our man-made religious fences ....

Steve

I had been praying the passage from John 1:35–9, in which Jesus invites two of John's disciples to 'come and see' where he lives and what he is about, when my journey to 'come and see' took on a life of its own, in a wholly unexpected moment.

It was 4 p.m., in the Market Square. A warm, sunny afternoon. I had collected my daughter from school and we were walking between the market stalls. As we walked, I noticed a man whose sad, child-like face caught my attention. As we passed him, he held out his hand and asked if I had any cigarettes. I hadn't. I shook my head and walked on.

We stopped to buy ice-creams and sat on a bench in the sun to eat them. The minutes passed and my thoughts were haunted by the sad face of the man I had passed by, and failed. I had to go back. I had to find him.

He had moved on. Eventually I found him near the multi-storey car park. Sitting at the roadside. Hoping and despairing alternately. I crouched down beside him and we talked for a while. It wasn't easy to understand him through the intoxication and the crying. But I could see the main characters in his drama: an abandoned child; an alcoholic; a server of sentences; a searcher for home.

He told me that his name was Steve. I told him that mine was Margaret. We had shared our names and entered into some kind of contract with each other.

I fetched him something to eat from the nearby baker's. He clutched it eagerly and as he took it, it occurred to me that it had cost me less than our ice-creams. I felt suddenly sick about the discrepancy.

'Where do you sleep?' I asked him. It was a rash question. I hadn't thought about the consequences of what the answer might be. He looked straight into my eyes, and stood up, rocking, and unsteady. *'Come and see'*, was his reply. A stab of panic shot through me, and I heard the voice of Jesus ringing out the unmistakable challenge.

Inwardly I took a determined step back from him, as he pointed down to the dark, deserted basement of the multi-storey car park. Even in his alcoholic haze – perhaps because of it – he sensed my hesitation. 'You're afraid, aren't you?' he said. I was silent for a few moments. My mind searched feverishly for appropriate excuses, and tried to suppress the rising realisation that I didn't really want to know at all where he slept, and that my question had been merely a polite pleasantry.

He urged me again to *'come and see'*. I thought of Jesus. I remembered that at 4 p.m. he too had been entertaining unexpected guests and answering thoughtless questions. The memory of him left me no choice. I followed Steve down to his 'home', his mattress on the concrete floor in a dark, stinking corner.

We stayed there for a few minutes together, while he ate his little meal and showed me his kingdom. His tears flowed and his nose ran. As he took the handkerchief I gave him, his penetrating blue eyes met mine, and I knew that I had discovered where Jesus lives. There was no need to search my imagination. The reality was here at my feet, on a mouldy mattress with an empty bottle and a runny nose.

Maggie Martin's Christmas Tree

Strange, that I had never taken any particular notice before of the Christmas Tree in the presbytery, even though the priest (let's call him Mark), whose tree it was, had lived there for nine years. But I did notice it this year, at the time of the children's Christmas Mass. It stood there in the corner of the room, lovingly decorated, and twinkling with pinpoints of fairy light. In the adjacent corner, Sarah sat in the rocking chair with her baby David in her arms, gently rocking back and forth to the rhythm of the carols. Between her and the tree, Mark had set up the altar and the candles were lit. Children and parents were clustered around it.

It was quite by chance, the next day, in a conversation with Mark, that I heard about the origins of the tree. He had come upon Maggie Martin when he was looking after a poverty-torn parish in inner London. She had called him one night in the small hours and he had responded to her cry for help by setting off into the night, equipped with the means to administer the last rites if necessary, only to find her the worse for wine and even more the worse for loneliness. It was the first of many such encounters.

Maggie was well into her forties. She had been married and divorced three times, after which she had dispensed with the formalities. 'I'd come to Confession, Father,' she would say, 'but I know that if a man knocked at the door I'd be in bed with him as soon as wink.' She knew prison from the inside, but the comforts of the Church she could only gaze at from outside, her face pressed up against the window of respectability. But when the presbytery was burgled, her faith was absolute: 'It wasn't one of the lads, Father. I've told them not to touch the presbytery.'

One Christmas, she had a row with her lover. Things got rough and feelings ran high. She threw him out into the street and the Christmas Tree, his gift to her, out with him. The rejected lover slunk off into the night, leaving her to cool her temper in the frosty air and to reflect that perhaps it was a shame to waste the tree. She didn't want it back. That would be like taking the lover back. But it was a shame to waste it. There was a knock at the presbytery door, and Mark was given the tree, together with its decorations and an honest account of how she had come to part with it.

Christmas Eve came, and the tree, lovingly decorated, stood in the presbytery hall. Mark called on its previous owner and invited her to come and see how beautiful it looked. She admired it, content that in some accidental sort of way the right thing had been done, but honesty compelled confession: 'I ought to warn you, Father, they're all nicked, the decorations.'

Little by little, the great divide between Maggie's world and Mark's shrank. She started to respect the man who was respecting her. They recognised the Christ in each other and acknowledged between them a part in bringing him to birth. She started to bring herself, her despair and her hope to Mass, and he, in return, invited her to try a different, more sustaining kind of wine.

Maggie died of cancer when she was fifty. Before she died she wrote these words to Mark, who, like the Lord he follows, had the grace and the courage to cross over to the world beyond the pale:

'I came late to the faith
A stranger, searching
From sorrow seeking
Solace, where it hid;
An outsider, face pressed
Against the window
Looking in . . ..

And it seemed that
I was bade,
"Enter, and be still."
And in the celebration
Of the blessed bread and wine,
I saw a hand of friendship.
And I heard:
"In this sweet oasis,
take your fill."'

Whenever I read them I think of how Mark has lovingly set up that tree year by year ever since she first brought it to him – how he has adorned it with its stolen decorations and remembered, as he has done so, a sad, broken, defiant face, pressed up against the window, and then a face ravaged by the last stages of cancer, and finally the face that fought and battled and found at last the peace in the eye of the storm.

The tree stands there now, each Christmas, shining in the presbytery window, with a kind of death-defying joy and an irrational hopefulness that makes a fool of the logic of despair. It stands for itself, but it stands there for Maggie, riddled with sin and full of grace, who had the courage to say 'Yes' in the ghetto, and bring God to birth in a London slum.

The words of consecration are spoken. Maggie's labour, Maggie's sin and sorrow are offered up in token of us all. Sarah still rocks her son to and fro in the candleglow, and children and parents respond . . . . 'Lord I am not worthy to receive you, but only say the Word . . . .'

And the Word is made flesh, and dwells among us, full of grace and truth. And we behold his glory, twinkling in stolen fairy lights, and flickering in broken hearts, until the Dawn.

Adam the child-killer

I have changed Adam's name and the details of his story, but he was real enough, and he had the courage to appear on a TV documentary called *Killing in Common*. The programme was a series of interviews with people who, for all kinds of different reasons, had taken another human life. Some has been responsible for a fatal accident, others had been involved in more deliberate actions. Adam had killed his own child and he had done so with deliberate intention. But let him tell his own story . . . .

Adam and his wife Grace (I have chosen their 'names' with care) had longed for a child. When she was born, it became clear that she was disastrously damaged, both mentally and physically. Her parents and doctors considered the situation and discussed all the possibilities. They came to the conclusion that it would not be right to keep the baby artificially alive indefinitely, but that they would provide her merely with warmth and ventilation and let her die naturally. This process, they believed, would take only a day or two, and she would slip away from them painlessly.

Three agonising weeks later, the baby was still alive, and her parents were still keeping vigil at the cot-side. Then came the moment when Adam's heart snapped open, and his endurance was at an end. For a few moments he was alone with his daughter, while his wife went out and the nurse was elsewhere. He quickly disconnected the ventilator. Almost immediately the baby's heart monitor registered alarm, and the nurse came rushing in. She recognised the baby's terminal distress and its cause, and picked her up out of her cot. Then she looked deep into Adam's eyes, and her heart melted. 'Would you like to hold her?' she asked him. 'I would', he said, as he took the little girl into his arms, where she died a few moments later.

Adam was interviewed for the programme, and asked, inevitably, how he had felt at that moment. He admitted frankly that he had no belief in God or in an after-life and was in no way a 'religious' man, but, he went on: 'At that moment I knew a power of love that I had never ever known before. I loved her totally, even as I took her life.' His voice faltered as he spoke, before the cameras, and his eyes filled with tears, yet all who saw him knew that he had discovered real peace in that moment where love and grief had embraced in his heart and locked him in an eternal bond of love, both with his tiny daughter and with her maker.

The words of the hymn floated back to me, as I watched: 'Did e'er such love and sorrow meet, or thorns compose so rich a crown?' Adam probably never knew the hymn, but he knew its meaning, and he shared something of that knowledge with all who shared in his epiphany of love during that programme.

God comes to meet us where we dare not walk ourselves.

The prophet margins

The world is teeming with Steves and Maggies and Adams. If your heart has found the way across the causeway that connects your life of prayer with your life in the streets and factories and estates around you, you will know for yourself some of the people who beckon you to take your believing beyond the pale.

How will you respond?

Might it be that some kind of a revolution is called for, not in the hungry, aching world, but in *us*, the believers in God and followers of his Way? I have a mental picture of the power of God that could be described, perhaps, as a ball of fire with a thin crust surrounding it. The power breaks through that crust at the points where the crust is weakest. I know that I can say, with conviction, that this power has become effective in my own life at *my* weakest points, and I know too that those who have ministered

Our fences can never
enclose The Way, but they
can block our vision of it.

to my spiritual journey most effectively have done so out of their own experience of brokenness and vulnerability.

This observation about the nature of God's power might cause us to reflect very carefully and prayerfully on how we are called to respond to this calling from those who are 'beyond the pale'. We might discover that it is not we who are bringing the Gospel to them, but they to us. God's power, as we all acknowledge, was seen at its most invincible when his own Son hung, a mangled corpse, in a place of execution. And that Son himself told us to seek and find him among the outcast and the downcast. It would be at the weakest points in the thin crust of our society, he told us, that the power of love would be able to break through to us most authentically.

Far from being the 'unconverted' whom we must pull back into 'the fold of the church' on our own terms and conditions, these people on the margins are prophets of God's power, the first places where that power breaks through into the life of the world, if only we will open our eyes to see and open our ears to listen. We have more to learn from them, by far, than they from us. But to learn we must listen, and to come close enough to listen, we must have the courage to step beyond the pale. And if we don't know how to do this, we have One who teaches us by his own example. An excellent way of getting in touch with this lived example is to pray the Gospels imaginatively, in the way suggested in Chapter 13. But then to take what we have learned in prayer out into the world in which we live our lives.

Full circle

And so prayer becomes a circular journey – a circle, which like the circle of the Trinity itself, embodies every one of our lived and living relationships. We may begin this journey in the hope of deepening our relationship with God in personal prayer, and seeking to know ourselves more truly within that relationship with God. But the journey will not let us rest until the circle is completed, and the whole of creation discovers what it means to be fully alive.

Every time we return from the heights of prayer back to the life that lies both within and beyond the pale of our experience, we are re-enacting the Incarnation. We are doing what Jesus did, entering the sweat and blood and tears of life when it would be so much more appealing to stay in the ivory tower of prayer. Perhaps this is one way in which we are called to play our part in drawing the full circle of God's love around the creation in which that love is expressed.

TAKING IT FURTHER ...

I met God at the fish van one Friday morning. As I was making my purchase, I became aware of a rather sweet and smiling elderly lady in the process of selecting a trout. She seemed like the epitome of all that is wholesome and good-natured in a human community, and I warmed to her.

Then my smile turned into a peal of (suppressed) laughter, as she gazed trustfully at the fishmonger and expressed her request: 'Please will you decapitate it for me? I don't like the way it looks at me!'

The whole incident was just one of those things that lighten the heaviness of everyday, and I might have left it at that, had I not, at that moment, been visited by an inner vision of Herod, ordering the beheading of John the Baptist, for no better reason than that his niece 'didn't like the way he looked at her'.

So there I was, side by side with God in the market place, and there were a few searching questions to be answered:

- Have you ever tried to do that? To get rid of a person who was bearing some kind of reproach against you that you preferred not to look at? You may not have gone as far as beheading, but what about all those other ways of 'cutting someone stone dead'?
- Have you ever side-lined someone who represents what is uncomfortable to live with? Have you walked past a Steve, or despised a Maggie Martin, or condemned an Adam?
- Have you fallen into the habit of finding ways to eliminate or side-step what needs to be corrected in your life, rather than having the courage to look it in the eye? And is this habit becoming a way of life?

You might like to reflect on them yourself.

Some weeks after the encounter at the fish van, the daily reading (in Luke 9:7–9) brought me up against Herod again. This time he was pondering on who on earth this 'Jesus' might be, who was causing such a stir, and wondering uneasily whether the popular rumours might contain any truth that this could be John the Baptist, risen from the dead. 'John?' he says. 'I beheaded him. So who is this that I hear such reports about?'

And it is true, isn't it? We may cut off the head of what is looking at us with reproach, but it will come back again and again, in so many different shapes, until we face it in honest humility and let it say what it has to say.

Reflect on anyone you know who is 'beyond the pale' in whatever way: perhaps alienated from the Church or from society, or marginalised in some form. What can you learn from this person? How might you enter into a more creative and mutually respectful relationship with that person?

A powerful book which introduces the reader to a number of people whose life experience has driven them beyond the margins in extreme suffering is *Good Friday People* by Sheila Cassidy (Darton, Longman and Todd, 1991).

26. PRAYER UNCEASING?

Letting prayer become a way of life

We have come to the end of our journey together, but I hope that it is true to say that what we have actually done is to come to the end of the *beginning* .... And if the reflections we have shared have been, in any sense, a new beginning, or a start-off point into ways of prayer you may not have tried before, where would you like this beginning to lead you from now on?

We might describe this journey as a time when we have looked at the map together, and read the brochures. We have seen some of the pictures in the brochure, and heard a little about ways of travelling and various landmarks along the way. Some of the places in the brochure may not interest us much, while others make us feel we really would like to go there and discover the place in our own way. If any of the ways of experiencing prayer, that we have looked at, make you feel like that, then listen to that invitation in your heart to go further, dig deeper, discover for yourself what prayer may be opening up for you in a renewed and personal relationship with God.

The Music Box

As we plod on with our daily lives, it's easy to lose sight of what treasure we can discover in our own hearts when we connect them to the heart of God in prayer. I remember feeling very much like this one year at the end of a retreat, and wondering how I could hope to keep the joy of prayer alive through what often seems like the drudgery of common day. Perhaps God was reading my thoughts, because when I went into the chapel for the final Eucharist, I was delighted and surprised to hear some unusual music ....

For the first time in eight days I arrived in the chapel five minutes early. It felt good to be able to take my place quietly and serenely and re-collect myself for a few minutes and listen to the music. Usually it was something meditative, a Taizé chant perhaps, but today it surprised me. The sound of a delicate tinkling music box tune emerged, and it captured my imagination more than I would have expected. It almost set my feet tapping and it filled me with a funny kind of joy.

I listened attentively, and I felt as if the Lord was sitting next to me, leaning over towards me, rather impishly, and whispering: '*See! You play a tune.*' I didn't need to ponder the strange comment for long. As soon as he 'said' it I felt the power of its truth and I could see just what he meant.

I saw myself sitting for what seems like forever, simply turning my life's handle day after day after day. Most of the time it seems completely pointless. It gets me nowhere fast. It makes my arm ache and it makes my heart ache. It makes me feel used, and useless, and boring and bored. The picture put my life in a nutshell, and I suspected that I wasn't the only one sitting there in the chapel who might feel like that.

But into all of my musing, that whispered comment broke through like a sudden rainbow in a downcast sky. '*See! You play a tune.*'

I listened again to the tinkling melody. It really is true. My endless handle-turning and apparently pointless daily grind is somehow connected to the sweet, plaintive melody coming out of the box. A simple, almost mechanistic melody, to be sure, but it has a charm and it gladdens my heart.

I let it take me through some of the points of our meetings during the retreat. It took me to the furze-covered hillside, and the seed-pods, exploding with life in the summer sun, joined their noise to it. The rabbits came out of their burrows and leapt among the grassy tussocks. The wind joined in and a storm-tossed raven swooped into the chorus. The gurgling voice of the river sang the descant as it wound its way down to the estuary, and the sweeping constellations of the black nights provided the full supporting orchestra.

Before the tape ended and the service began, I had let my heart be swept up into this amazing Hallelujah Chorus. And my tune was in there too, cherished by its creator and amplified a hundredfold until all creation sang it with me as I sang with theirs.

It slowed, steadied and stopped, momentarily out of breath. But it had made me see my daily grind a little differently and it had deepened my love and reverence for the contents of that black box, planted by God somewhere in the centre of my heart, that turns my grinding into music.

Something similar came alive for me one bleak grey day in the ruined nave of Coventry Cathedral, which was destroyed by bombing in the Second World War. In the bell tower the bell-ringers were ringing out the call to Evensong. I watched them, through the glass walls of their ringers' platform.

All that each of them was doing (so it seemed to my untutored eyes) was heaving one thick rope up and down, yet the result was a joyous peal that resounded across the city. Sometimes such a peal was a call to prayer and praise, as it was that evening. Sometimes it was an overflowing of celebration, or the steady, inevitable tolling of grief. Perhaps it rang out here in terror as the bombs rained down in 1941. Perhaps it pealed in broken thankfulness when the cease-fire was declared in 1945. Or in the surge of new birth in 1962 when the cathedral was re-dedicated.

Prayer – and life! – can feel like this. The laboured, apparently meaningless, often dry repetition. The pull on the rope that hurts our hands. Can there be any connection with the peal of the response of all creation in which, mysteriously, we have a part? Can our monotone of meditation be part of the universal chord that searches achingly around the universe until it finds the Word of which it is the echo? I believe it can. My heart knows that it *is*.

Praying continuously?

It's easy, and very natural, to come to the end of a journey like this full of enthusiasm and determination to keep going. We probably all know, from past experience, that this period of enthusiasm can be short-lived, and yet, as St Paul tells us, we are called into a lasting – an *everlasting* – relationship with the Lord where we are to 'pray at all times'.

I used to think that St Paul must have been living on a different planet when he urged the Thessalonians to 'pray continually'. Then, one day, a friend told me a little story about something that had happened to him. He had been making a journey that had led him past a bird sanctuary. Having plenty of time to spare, he had decided to stop off and spend a few hours there in the peace and quiet of a 'hide', where he would do a bit of bird-watching, and relax at the same time. He went on to tell me how he had made his way to the hide, and how, before he had even reached the hide, a stranger had approached him and drawn his attention to the distant call of a bittern, quite a rare bird on these islands.

I was very impressed, and was telling a colleague at work about the incident. Now my colleague is, one might say, a *real* bird-watcher, not just a visitor who spends an afternoon in the nature reserve. He takes his hobby very seriously. Family holidays mean tents and binoculars, whatever the weather! Anyway, as I was telling him about my friend's encounter with the bittern, he interrupted me with the words: 'No, it's not like that. You don't go into the hide and then start listening. *You listen all the time*, and some of the listening may happen to be done from inside the hide.' Something in what he said made me think of prayer. I found myself feeling quite excited and eager to hear more about this full-time listening, and the secrets it might reveal.

'If you are really interested in the world of birds,' he told me, 'you gradually become *permanently* tuned in to the birdsong. You start to notice every change of tone and pitch and to understand its meaning. More than that, you notice the absence of certain notes, or certain birds even. You notice patterns and subtle changes in the orchestration. What you hear starts to make you aware of a whole landscape of life that is totally other than your own, yet totally connected.' It sounded more and more like prayer. I thought of how prayer tunes us in to the kingdom of God, which is still totally 'other' to us in our fallen state, yet to which we are so deeply connected.

That night I lay in bed thinking over what I had heard. I thought back over the day I had just lived through. From my first waking moments, God had been singing me his signals, in the people I had met, the things I had experienced, the world I had lived in. It was God who was holding it all in being and there was nothing in my day that was not capable of revealing to me some aspect of its creator . . . if only I could learn to listen! When I looked at it this way, my own efforts seemed to get in the way. My determination to 'pray properly' was actually disturbing the very stillness that would make space for the birdsong.

There is a place for effort. We need to spend time, as it were, 'in the hide', to train our inner ears to hear the fullness of God's voice. We do need to practise stilling ourselves, and focusing our hearts on God and on his Word in very deliberate ways, like the ones we have been looking at together. But the greater reality of prayer is to be in touch with the world that the birdsong reveals, to be in tune with God in every moment of our lives and to find him in everything and everyone around us. And in time we will become increasingly still, inwardly, whatever we are doing at the time. We will start to hear God's heartbeat throbbing through everything he has created.

It is this *desire*, I believe, that will keep us 'going on'. If the journey onwards depends on our self-discipline and determination and will-power, it will probably founder and fail. But if it is fuelled by our real and deep desire to be close to God, then it has every chance of growing in depth and in joy and bringing us daily closer to our home in the Lord. It will become like a plant with a deep root, that doesn't depend on the passing weather to stay alive, but draws its nourishment from the ground water, that never fails.

And so I invite you to look at prayer, and your own desire for prayer, through the eyes of my bird-watcher colleague. Let your prayer be drawn gently forward by your *desire* and not driven by your sense of duty. 'Pray as you can, and not as you can't' is sound advice. Choose the ways of prayer that help you personally to draw close to God. Be realistic about how long you can spend 'in the hide' (that is, deliberately in prayer) each day, and try to find that time if you possibly can. Far better to make a space of ten minutes for God and keep to it than to try to meditate for an hour at a stretch and then feel guilty because it doesn't work out as you had hoped. In fact I would go so far as to say that guilt of this kind *has no place in prayer*. All that it does is sap your energy and diminish the quality of your relationship with God. So let it go, and good riddance to it! Let God liberate you from such false guilt.

And when you think that your time 'in the hide' is over, remember that when you leave 'the hide' (that is, when you are not actually 'in prayer' in any recognisable way), you are living your daily life out in the wide world, open to the song of God in every moment and in every interaction with his people and his world. Like the music box, the daily grind of your life is producing its own constant music, that perhaps only others can hear. This, I believe, is what it means to 'pray continually'. The prayer that looks back over the events of the day, seeking God's touch in all that has happened, is probably the most effective key to this continual awareness of God in your life, and alertness to his guiding. And another great help in keeping your friendship with God alive and well is to share something of your experience of the journey regularly with a trusted friend, or with a small group of people with whom you feel comfortable.

'Faith is the bird who
sings while dawn is still dark',
and prayer is her heart's song.

Just before the dawn chorus begins, while it is still dark, in the early hours of a summer morning, there is a single, solitary bird-call. This is the herald of the dawn. I would like to leave you with the thought that your personal prayer, whatever form it may take, is like that first call of your soul to God, and it is the herald of a dawn that will one day fulfil and surpass your wildest hopes and expectations. Not just for yourself, but for the whole human family. For faith, it is said, is the bird who sings while dawn is still dark, and prayer is her heart's song.

Flowers of the night

And speaking of the darkness before the dawn makes me think of the flowers of the night, who open their petals as dusk falls, and attract the pollinating moths by means of scent rather than sight.

Prayer seems to me a bit like that. We live our daylight lives, busy, or bored, active or incapacitated, in a world of visibility. In prayer we move into a still and silent place in the darkness of our own hearts. Prayer, I am convinced, releases a fragrance within us, though we never realise it, which in turn has the power to attract others to its source in God.

When I come home from work and greet my cat, I know exactly where he has been, by the scent of his fur. I know at once whether he has spent the day in the newly manured field, or in the pile of freshly laundered clothes. He takes on the scent of wherever he has spent his time and he carries that scent with him round the house. I think we do the same, but in less obvious ways. We take on the scent of whatever we choose to be close to. If our hearts live mainly with what is negative, inturned or destructive, this will somehow infuse us with the 'smell' of such things. But every minute we spend in prayer, consciously close to God, will soak us in his fragrance. We will never know that this has happened, but others will! They will catch the scent of God on our lives, and be attracted to it.

Faith, perhaps, is this: a joy caught from closeness to God, and carried into an aching world. We 'catch' this joy in prayer, whatever form prayer takes, and we carry it, unconsciously like night flowers, in our lives.

And so I pray, from my heart, for God's blessing upon your journey and for the light, the warmth and the fragrance of his grace and his love upon your dawn.

ADDRESSES

To make contact with a faith-sharing network in your area, contact:

Mr John McGlinchey
1st Floor
Champleys Mews
Market Place
Pickering
North Yorkshire
YO18 7AE

Ms Teresa House
Christian Life Community
St Joseph's
Watford Way
London
NW4 4TY